PLANNING, BUDGETING, AND CONTROL FOR DATA PROCESSING

How to Make Zero Base Budgeting Work for You

PLANNING, BUDGETING, AND CONTROL FOR DATA PROCESSING

How to Make Zero Base Budgeting Work for You

Thomas J. Francl
W. Thomas Lin
Miklos A. Vasarhelyi

VNR VAN NOSTRAND REINHOLD COMPANY

Library of Congress Catalog Card Number: 83-10417
ISBN: 0-442-22550-4

Manufactured in the United States of America

Published by Van Nostrand Reinhold Company Inc.
135 West 50th Street
New York, New York 10020

Van Nostrand Reinhold Company Limited
Molly Millars Lane
Wokingham, Berkshire RG11 2PY, England

Van Nostrand Reinhold
480 Latrobe Street
Melbourne, Victoria 3000, Australia

Macmillan of Canada
Division of Gage Publishing Limited
164 Commander Boulevard
Agincourt, Ontario M1S 3C7, Canada

15 14 13 12 11 10 9 8 7 6 5 4 3 2 1

Library of Congress Cataloging in Publication Data

Francl, Thomas J.
Planning, budgeting, and control for data processing.

Bibliography: p.
Includes index.
1. Electronic data processing departments—Management.
2. Management information systems. 3. Management—Data processing. 4. Zero-base budgeting. I. Lin, W. Thomas. II. Vasarhelyi, Miklos A. III. Title.
IV. Title: M.I.S. planning, budgeting, and control.
HF5548.2.F719 1984 658'.054 83-10417
ISBN 0-442-22550-4

To my wife, partner, and best friend, Charlene Francl.
To my loving Wife, Angela Hou Lin.
To Marina Vasarhelyi.

Biographies

Thomas J. Francl is president of TIF Associates in Arcadia, California. He received a B.S. from Loyola University in Chicago and an M.B.A. in accounting from the University of Southern California. He holds a Certificate in Management Accounting (C.M.A.) and is an adjunct assistant professor at California State University, Los Angeles. He has over 14 years of data processing management and technical experience and has authored several systems articles.

W. Thomas Lin is an associate professor of accounting at the University of Southern California. He received a B.A. from National Taiwan University, an M.S. from the University of California, Los Angeles, and a Ph.D. from Ohio State where he also taught accounting. He is a C.M.A. and has published many articles in accounting and systems journals.

Miklos A. Vasarhelyi is an associate professor of accounting at Columbia University. He earned a B.S. from the Catholic University of Rio de Janeiro, an M.S. degree from MIT, and a Ph.D. from the University of California, Los Angeles. The former director of the Rio Datacenter, Dr. Vasarhelyi has published three books and many articles on accounting subjects.

Preface –The Unanticipated

How often has your company's executive reacted to your latest hardware request like this: "What do you mean, we need another string of 3380 disks? We just installed two of them last month!" Or, when was the last time you reacted to the vice president of Marketing like this: "Sorry, we can't get to your market survey project for at least six months. My programmers are all tied up." Sound familiar? Sadly, most MIS* managers are faced with these situations every day and continue to lose the respect of their boss and their peers.

That all of us in data processing are faced with these pressures and that most of us react the same way is not very comforting. If we really want to be successful in our careers and make significant contributions to our employers, we must be better than average MIS managers. We must try harder than our peers in the operating departments because, in most instances, we are still looked upon as mere technicians. There are many things we can do to alleviate this stereotyping. We can become better educated about our company and business in general. Many of us have gone back to school to earn the bachelor's degree or even an M.B.A. Many of us have forced ourselves to get out of the everyday bits and bytes to the point where we not only don't know the difference between RPG II and RPG III but don't even care.

In this book, what we are suggesting is that a good quality planning process can do wonders for our problems. The unanticipated projects and production volume increases will be drastically reduced to the point that we will be able to calmly and rationally address each one. If the process is well established, that vice president of Marketing will no longer be able to point the finger at the lack of internal data processing support for his or her million dollar project. In fact, that VP is the one who will come across as being unprepared. Wouldn't it be great to have the vice presidents of Finance, Operations, and Personnel on *your* side for a change?

---

*Management Information Systems

No, the authors do not have a miracle cure or the perfect solution to your problem. In this book we are attempting to apply a different twist to the basic planning process. The use of *zero base budgeting* is not new but is presented here in light of the unique problems of data processing. If you get back to basics with the disciplines outlined herein, the odds are two to one that your job will be a lot easier and possibly even enjoyable.

We are extremely thankful to Charlene Francl for the motivation she supplied throughout the long and sometimes tedious process of writing this book. We are also grateful to her for her many suggestions and proofreading efforts.

Thomas J. Francl
W. Thomas Lin
Miklos A. Vasarhelyi

Contents

1
Strategic Planning

Planning within MIS has become a very important subject within the past few years, primarily because operating department managers, under increased budgetary pressures, have become more sophisticated and have begun to produce sophisticated plans for their own operations and to use more advanced management tools. MIS managers are being forced to keep up and even take the lead because of the very nature of their operations. Still, *plan* is a four letter word in a great many companies. These companies are typically small organizations run by entrepreneurs who are more interested in getting the job done rather than sitting around discussing it. They do not like formal policies and procedures and hence do not engage in the "bureaucratic" process of planning. In large organizations where formal planning has been the status quo for years, functional planning is being moved down into lower levels of management and managers are now forced to learn the process. It is evident that planning is a company-wide activity and not just something that MIS needs to do. If your company does not practice the art of *strategic planning* or even annual *operational planning,* your work is cut out for you. But do not give up before you start. Being one of the few well-administered departments in the company has significant advantages and will place you one step ahead of your peers in the eyes of top management.

Two issues should be kept in mind as we walk through the planning process: the MIS plan is not a stand-alone document that is completed in a vacuum. On the contrary, the MIS plan must complement the corporate plan and must be integrated with the individual operating department plans. Second, the MIS plan, as described in this book, is not to be filed on the shelf only to be referenced during next year's planning cycle. It should become a real, live tool of control and direction that governs the actions of the department throughout the year and, if necessary, should be updated throughout the year.

Chapter 1 concentrates on planning over a two to five year time period while the next chapter discusses the immediate planning period. Zero base budgeting (ZBB) is emphasized throughout this process because it is so well suited to data processing. Chapter 3 details the contents of a ZBB decision package while Chapter 4 recommends a method of ranking those packages. Then, in Chapter 5, a traditional budget is prepared in light of the results of the ranking process. Chapter 6 discusses how to control expenses during the year. Because the zero base budgeting process can be labor-intensive, the final two chapters suggest ways of automating the decision packages and other uses for the information. The package preparation effort can be reduced and the features of the ZBB process are capitalized upon which will provide an additional return on your investment.

This introductory chapter discusses the importance, definition, and benefits of strategic planning in the MIS department. It covers the three components of a typical strategic plan: corporate plans, operating department plans, and MIS department plans. It then describes the process of conducting an analysis of our weaknesses, strengths, threats, opportunities, MIS goals, and plans and programs. Next, the resource requirements, a sample time schedule, and a sample report are presented. Finally, the chapter suggests that new MIS managers should start to think about adopting a new strategic planning process during the first few months.

Strategic planning is defined as the long-range planning process that typically covers a 2 to 5 year time span. It is contrasted with futures research, which extends 20 to 30 years in the future and is therefore only practiced by the very large corporations. It is also contrasted with operational planning which is limited to the 1-year cycle that coincides with a company's fiscal year and budget cycle.

Long-range project planning is not the same as strategic planning. Project planning is included in the strategic plan on an aggregate level. In the operational plan, specific projects are included in some detail.

Nolan (1973b) found that planning, especially strategic planning, is not implemented within MIS until it is usually too late. Planning is usually introduced during the third stage, which he refers to as the *control stage,* when it should be implemented in stage I, the *initiation stage.*

Strategic planning must become a integral part of the MIS planning process. Too often, we are rudely awakened to the fact that the last time a five-year plan was prepared was five years ago. If this describes your situation, you are probably the typical MIS manager. You are action-oriented, understand how SNA differs from X.25, and waste no time with paperwork. Your nickname is probably "Unprepared Phil," just like our ficticious vice president of Marketing (see the Preface).

Long-range planning, the key to your success, requires you to look beyond the edge of your desk. If long-range planning in your department consists of trying to figure out what is going to happen tomorrow, you are too entrenched in detail. Start delegating by letting your staff take care of the daily operational problems. If you do not trust them, either you have not given them the proper training or they are incapable. As the MIS manager, you cannot be expected to resolve operating system hard loops or payroll systems that are out-of-balance.

In summary, then, what are you going to get out of all of this planning effort? Plenty, especially if your MIS department does not currently go through a formal planning process. If you currently have a formal process in place, this chapter may give you additional insight and suggestions. Even if this is your very first attempt at putting together a strategic plan, the benefits will still be tremendous:

- Improved communications not only with your end users but also within your own MIS department. If you produce a good plan, everyone you deal with on a day-to-day basis will know where you are headed and in what time frame. There will be no surprises to them or to you. Spur-of-the-moment projects can either be absorbed by planned slack or postponed until the next formal planning cycle.
- Projects with a high return on investment (ROI) are identified and scheduled to begin before those with marginal returns. If your company is driven by bottom-line results, the ROI of a project takes precedence over a user's pet project.
- Coordinated systems development is a natural by-product of the strategic planning process. All major projects are identified and scheduled in relation to one another. The process lends itself to true information management (sometimes referred to as *data administration*). With proper planning, data redundancy and inconsistencies disappear.

- Better understanding of the company and the operating departments is an obvious benefit. As data processing professionals who frequently change jobs and industries, we need to understand whom we are working for. Every company has its own personality and ways of doing business, even those within the same industry or city.
- Ignoring current production problems allows you and your staff to look at the "ideal" and escape from today's world. Each user department or division is analyzed whether they currently utilize your services or not. New ideas on how to meet previously unidentified needs are generated and welcomed by the end users.

Before you begin the strategic planning process, be sure that everyone is committed: your staff, your management, and especially yourself. It will be up to you to sell them on these ideas, so your commitment is the most important. It will do more harm than good to produce a half-baked, shoddy document than to produce none at all.

THE STRATEGIC PLAN

The MIS strategic plan is comprised of three main sections: corporate plans, operating department plans, and MIS department plans. The assumption is made that the corporate and operating department plans either do not exist or are not detailed enough for your use. If they are perfect, then your job is greatly simplified.

The corporate plan section must contain topics similar to the following:

- Current/proposed markets
- Current/proposed products
- Market share
- Service levels
- Position toward government regulation
- Employee composition
- Industrialization
- Industry trends

Although it is extremely difficult, if not impossible, for the MIS staff to write such a plan, you must at least investigate and understand these topics. If your company is a manufacturer local to the Midwest and plans an expansion to the East Coast, for example, the impact upon MIS can be tremendous: data communications, a remote data center, distributed processing, and so on. If the company plans to double its market share, are you going to have a hardware capacity problem?

The operating department plan and the MIS plan are similar in nature. They both contain mission statements, significant strategies, and programs for implementation. The operating department plans must be produced before the MIS plan is completed under the assumption that MIS is a service organization and not the chief executive.

It must be emphasized that the strategic plan is not merely a list of projects and the corresponding resources needed to implement them. On the contrary, the strategic plan is driven by overall objectives and desired results and says nothing about how they will be accomplished. The strategic plan specifies what will be accomplished on a broad scale.

Do not limit your thought process. Letting your mind be creative is the fun part of the job. Avoid rationalizations like: "If only we could install another meg of memory, all our problems would be solved." Take the attitude that your resources and what you can create with them are unlimited. This is your opportunity to dream. Do not let the technicians shoot down an idea because it will use up additional CPU cycles. If your plan is good enough, you will justify double or triple your current hardware budget.

The development of the Plans and Programs section requires a great deal of creative thinking. In the formulation of these plans, you must conceptualize what MIS *ought* to be doing independent of what you are *actually* doing. The types of individuals involved in this creative process should not be uneducated persons of little experience with limited interests. They should be capable of logical, deductive reasoning and have a broad perspective of the company, the data processing industry, and life in general. A good systems analyst might qualify, but a systems programmer may not.

There are countless books and articles outlining how to prepare a departmental plan. Nolan (1973b) recommends an assessment of the growth stage before beginning the planning process. This assessment involves the analysis of:

1. *The applications portfolio:* The level of data processing support as compared to the company's needs.
2. *Data processing personnel and technology:* A review of the technical capabilities of the data processing area including hardware, software, and personnel.
3. *The User:* The experience level of the users is determined by the number of years and type of data processing applications they have been exposed to.
4. *Management controls:* Controls are needed for both the development and operation of systems.

The process outlined herein is simple and straightforward and, best of all, it works! The methodology is commonly referred to as a *WOTS-UP analysis* because it identifies the *Weaknesses, Opportunities, Threats* and *Strengths* facing the department. If you work for a small or medium-sized company, the analysis should be prepared for each department. In a large company, prepare the analysis for each division.

The WOTS-UP analysis should be kept as brief as possible preferably done in outline format. The major sections are described below:

Mission statement: What is the purpose of this department or division? What is its product or service? Why does it exist?

Weaknesses: What are the significant shortcomings of this department? For example, is it short of experienced personnel or are its personnel ignorant of what MIS can do for them (or to them). A word of caution, however: keep this section on a professional level. Do not try to condemn the department manager even if you think he is worthless. Keep in mind that this plan will be published for all to see. Remember you need his support in the preparation and acceptance of this report.

Strengths: What are the significant strong points of this department? Its members might be keenly aware of what data processing can do for them or it may have a strong management team, all of whom have MBAs and work unlimited amounts of overtime. The danger to avoid in this section is becoming too patronizing. Be honest and use the compliments only if they are deserved.

Threats: What factors could put this department or division out of business? Do they have trade secrets or sensitive client lists? Review the weaknesses to identify any that, if left to fester, could threaten the department.

Opportunities: How can this department best be served by MIS? Are there any threats or weaknesses that can be improved upon by proper systemization of departmental activities? Do not be too concerned about current workloads or MIS relationships with department management. Given unlimited resources, how can MIS best serve this department? Itemize major projects including those unapproved "pie in the sky" projects with little hope of approval.

MIS goals: Given the above analysis, how can MIS best serve this department. Remember that MIS is a support function, and we do not wish to even hint that we could do a better job running the department than the department's own people. Even if we could, we would want to position MIS itself as a true service operation. Can MIS provide significant cost savings by the automation of a certain process? Should MIS have dotted line responsibility over this division's own data processing department? Should MIS have no relationship with this group at all?

Plans and programs: Itemize exactly what MIS should do for this department. Look beyond those projects already approved, though do include them. Do not include projects already under way and do not limit yourself to only those projects that can be accomplished by your limited staff that is not familiar with X.25 or SNA.* What can be accomplished over the next few years given unlimited resources?

THE PROCESS

The most efficient way of conducting the planning process is to begin within your own department. Gather your management team together to analyze the MIS department. Examine your own house first and gain direct experience with the process. Explain the strategic

*X.25 and systems network architecture (SNA) are telecommunications protocols commonly used today. The former was adopted by the American National Standards Institute and the latter is marketed by IBM.

planning process and sample document to your staff. Explain to them what you are trying to accomplish and why. Let them read this chapter of the book. Prepare a WOTS-UP analysis using brainstorming techniques. Write down every idea on a black board, no matter how ridiculous you think it is. The key is to allow everyone to contribute freely and to build upon each other's ideas. Do not allow anyone to laugh at someone else's idea because that will be the last thing that individual contributes. After exhausting the particular section for ideas, capsulize them into six or seven concise statements that the majority of the group agrees upon.

Formulate the MIS mission statement into one paragraph. Agree upon a concise list of weaknesses, strengths, opportunities, and threats that is less than two pages in length. Try to be honest and open without appearing to be totally out of control. Skip the section entitled "MIS Goals." This part is only appropriate for the end user departments.

Complete the Plans and Programs section. Itemize those projects internal and unique to the MIS department that will enhance its effectiveness in meeting its objectives. For example, establishment of a quality assurance function or a hardware forecasting process might be appropriate.

After drafting the MIS section, begin analyzing the user departments. Look at their shortcomings and needs as well as their outstanding qualities. This part of the process is very time consuming and tiring. Several sessions will have to be scheduled to complete it. If the participants get weary and are short of ideas, continue the meeting at a later date.

Once you have drafted the WOTS-UP analysis for each department and division, have it typed, keeping each department separate. Make an appointment to meet with the principals of each department at which time you will explain your purpose and what you are trying to accomplish. Prepare another WOTS-UP analysis using yours as a guide but not as the bible. Confirm or deny each of your points because if you wrote them down initially, they have some importance. Each interview should last an hour or so and must stress the long term and not today's crises. After the preparation of the Plans and Programs section, agree upon the relative priority of each point and list them in that order. Handle this meeting as if you were a consultant. The department manager knows his business better than you do and you are merely trying to get his ideas documented. If he really does not know which end is up, steer him to your way of thinking or to that of the rest of the corporation.

After your initial interview, review your findings with your management team and discuss any significant discrepancies. Formally document the results of your interview and consensus in the WOTS-UP format. Send a copy to the department manager for approval. Make a statement in your cover memo that no one else has seen this document besides your staff and that this is his opportunity to modify it before publication, if necessary.

RESOURCES REQUIRED

The toughest part of future activities to sell is their associated cost. While nothing in life is free, no one wants to pay for data processing services if he can help it. Estimate hardware growth in terms of present-day usage. For example, if your accounts payable system uses three CPU hours a month, is it reasonable to assume that the proposed accounts receivable system will use a similar amount? Include in your hardware estimates sufficient disk space growth for present systems as well as the new ones. Be conservative and estimate hardware acquistion over the next five years at today's prices. We understand that hardware costs are dropping but they may not drop as rapidly in the next five years as they have in the last five.

Estimate the cost of staff based on any predicted growth in your department. Utilize large salary increase percentages because there is no end in sight to the shortage of qualified staff and their escalating salaries. Where appropriate, estimate the cost of software acquisition. While buying software packages is cheaper than writing your own software, the lump sum amounts can be staggering. Paying $70,000 for a fixed assets system is absurd but to produce the same system yourself would require several man years and a sum well in excess of $70,000.

TIME SCHEDULE

The preparation of the strategic plan and resulting operational plan can be so time consuming that it should be likened to a regular development project. A full 11 months of the year can be spent putting together your first MIS plan. This is 11 calendar months and should be much less than 11 man months. Large MIS departments allocate full-time staff to this planning effort. Establish a time schedule at the onset with assigned tasks and responsibilities. Hold regular status meetings to check the progress. The following time schedule should serve as an example for your use. Note that if your company has a regular planning process, you should adjust your schedule to it. This schedule assumes that your fiscal year is the calendar year.

January 1	Begin the WOTS-UP analysis within MIS. Revise last year's, if available.
February 1	Begin departmental interviews.
March 15	Strategic plan drafts returned to department heads.
April 1	Strategic plan published.
May 1	Strategic plan accepted by management.
August 1	Operational plan published.
September 1	Operational plan accepted by end user departments and management.
October 1	Next year's detailed budget submitted.
November 15	Budget approved.

SAMPLE REPORT

Reproduced in the Appendix to this chapter are portions of a long-range plan prepared for a medium-sized Los Angeles MIS department in 1981. A single WOTS-UP analysis is included for demonstration purposes. This plan included topics normally reserved for the operational plan because it was the first attempt to produce a true strategic plan for MIS.

NEW MIS MANAGERS

As an MIS manager recently promoted from within or as one that was recently hired from outside the company, you may very well be lost and groping for information. Why not use the techniques described above to get started? The WOTS-UP analysis is an excellent way of gathering information as well as getting to know the department managers. A tremendous benefit can be gained by just preparing the WOTS-UP analysis without publishing a full-blown strategic plan. It is a great way to get your feet on the ground fast.

Appendix
ABC Company
1981 MIS Strategic Plan

Table of Contents

LONG-RANGE PLAN

Mission Statement

The ABC Company is principally engaged in the transportation and warehousing of household goods, office and industrial equipment, electronic equipment, and business records. Additionally, other segments of the corporation provide janitorial maintenance, guard service, pest control, and furniture rental.

Management Information Services (MIS) provides the ABC Company and its subsidiaries with the information required to accomplish its strategic plans and tactical objectives, and to manage its operations effectively. In particular MIS will:

Direct the design of systems that provide management with the information necessary for planning, controlling, reporting, and decision making.

Provide staff direction to both corporate and operating-unit executives to ensure that data content and systems design meet management requirements.

Provide leadership in the effective use of internal data processing, office automation, telecommunication, and telephone equipment.

Provide data processing and communications services to ABC's organizational units.

Provide advice and counsel to corporate and operating unit executives.

Enhance ABC's profitability with cost effective solutions.

Manage information flows throughout the company, whether automated or not, and provide leadership for improvements where needed.

Establish a capability to back up the technical personnel at the remote sites.

Long-Range Direction

It is desirable that the data processing environment in a corporation mirror the overall organization. In the past, because of cost considerations, this was difficult to do. The large central processor, because of its ability to provide incrementally cheaper computation with increased size, became predominant. In most major corporations in the 1970s, one or a very small number of large computers typically performed all the data processing. Video and hard-copy terminals were attached to this processor(s) which thereby extended the machine capability to the staff. In the mid- to late-1970s, ABC was an example of this type of data processing environment.

ABC, however, is not a highly centralized company. The corporate staff is small, and the bulk of the responsibility resides with subsidiary management.

Because it is now economical to provide these subsidiaries with a data processing resource over which they can exercise more direct control, MIS has laid the groundwork for a layered computing environment, one with computer power at numerous locations throughout the company tied together with one or more networks over which information may be communicated.

Over the next few years, the environment can be viewed as consisting of four strata. The highest is the host or central processing layer from which overall control is exercised and from which a large processor(s) manages the machines installed at the various locations, controls the telecommunication network(s), and performs data processing for the corporate departments and those subsidiaries that do not wish to install their own machines.

The second layer is the network layer. The machines installed throughout the corporation will be interconnected by one or more telecommunication networks. These networks will be managed by machines located at the central site. Equipment will be installed in various out-of-state locations throughout the company. Voice switching systems will fall in this layer.

The satellite, or third layer, will be comprised of computer systems installed in subsidiary headquarters and branch offices. It is by these machines that the bulk of the satellite companies' computing will be performed. Users will be online to these machines and the bulk of the data processing will be interactive. These machines, although installed by the MIS organization, will be under the day-to-day control of the associated subsidiary.

Video, hard-copy, and other types of terminals make up the fourth layer. Many of these will be intelligent (microprocessors) and will perform edit and error rejection functions as well as small amounts of local processing. These will also be under the day-to-day control of the associated line organization.

FIVE-YEAR PLAN

Goals and Objectives

While the mission statement outlines those items that MIS should be engaged in, the five-year plan outlines those items that can be accomplished in the foreseeable future. The objectives that MIS will strive to achieve within the next five years include:

Provide low-cost solutions to information needs quickly.

Enhance voice and data communication to provide added capabilities.

Provide branch office systems that enhance efficient and cost-effective operations.

Provide for information sharing between systems and companies.

Provide direction for automation of central office clerical and routine management activities.

Shift more MIS responsibilities to the subsidiaries.

1983–1987 – The Distributed Period

These years will see the further distribution of functions away from the central computer facility even as the central facility takes on added importance because of its general-purpose capabilities and integrating influence.

Small microprocessor-based equipment or intelligent terminals will be installed in every major ABC office. These devices will be capable of communicating with one another, probably with the central facility acting as the hub. Data entry for each subsidiary will be localized. The smaller subsidiaries will have minicomputers located at their administrative centers. All these machines will be capable of communicating with one another, with the central site, and with out-of-state locations.

The central facility will still service the major divisions and the corporate office. The other subsidiaries will have elective access to the central site and may choose to do some processing there because of the availability of specialized software.

Additional main processor capacity must be installed. The IBM 370/158 must be enhanced by the first quarter of 1984. By the second quarter of 1985, it should be replaced.

During this period, emphasis will be on establishing proper balance between computer usage at the central facility and at the local offices. Standardization and integration of the remote systems will be emphasized.

MIS will be responsible for ensuring a stable evolution. It will add staff to provide new or expanded services in the areas of systems design and development, project management, quality assurance, data communication, and system and technical support.

The users' role will also undergo change. They will need to be increasingly able to identify business opportunities for automated systems and productivity improvements. They will be required to provide project management on some efforts. They must better understand their computer applications and they will be doing more and more of their own systems analysis work as generalized report writers and inquiry software become generally available.

This will be a period in which a high level of communication and cooperation will be required between MIS and the various subsidiaries. Corporate management will need to contribute heavily to ensure that goals are met, priorities established, and the appropriate level of resources made available to ensure ABC moves ahead of its competitors.

External data bases, the number of which is growing rapidly, may be useful to the ABC Company as new sources of business information not historically within

ABC. MIS will identify the offerings of the various vendors and make the results of the inquiry available to the operating companies.

Major Projects and Activities

Whereas MIS is a corporate support function, its activities are governed by the needs of the operating units. The medium-range activities that will meet these needs are defined by the corporate entity:

ABC Van Lines

Redesign old accounting systems to utilize the Waybill Accounting data base.

Develop information systems for special commodities, general commodities, fleet administration, marketing, and other company support areas.

Provide for flexible, user-defined reporting analyses of computerized data.

ABC Moving and Storage

Expand computerized functions to branch offices to include: data entry, report printing, integrated revenue data capture, distributed storage information, word processing, and financial modeling.

Provide for central office control of the distributed systems.

Provide voice communication direction.

Other Subsidiaries

Support local information-processing projects.

Provide financial modeling capabilities.

Provide technical consulting as required.

Provide voice communication direction.

Develop computerized links between these subsidiaries and corporate management.

Corporate Departments

Provide required systems.

Develop a low-cost, integrated office equipment structure to include word processing.

Provide computerized tools to management and staff to include financial modeling, data entry, and message transmission.

Management Information Systems

Revise system development procedures to take advantage of computerized aids.

Provide a mainframe computer resource that can be easily upgraded without major changes.

Continue to enhance the communication network.

Apply the latest proven technology to provide maximum computer availability to the users.

Organizational Implications

Computer Operations will not change significantly. The central facility may expand its hours to a full 24 hours a day, seven days a week, but the number and types of personnel will not change significantly.

Data Control will remain at about its current size.

Data Entry will be reduced in size as the end user organizations assume responsibility for their own entry of data.

Data Base will grow in importance as more and more corporate data is stored electronically in the computer. Safety and security will be increasingly important. Coupling the small remote computers with the central facility will require coordination of data base activities. This department will probably grow by 1986.

Telecommunications will have increasing importance to the company. The interconnection of the electronic hardware at the various offices will be the responsibility of this department. The staff will increase by one or two professionals.

Systems Software is responsible for maintaining the mainframe's operating system and, as these functions become more routine, the staff can be reduced by one professional. Support of the remotely installed hardware will be transferred to this department.

Systems and Programming should grow somewhat during this period. Perhaps more important than its growth will be its changing composition. Greater emphasis will be placed on business analysis and systems design and less upon programming because of the availability of productivity aids.

Distributed Data Processing requires more expertise in small computer systems and will also contribute heavily to office automation development and installation.

Quality Assurance should receive increasing importance as greater efforts are required in user training, project management, and standards development. However, because of financial constraints, this function may be reduced in size.

Subsidiaries will need to become increasingly aware of and capable of making use of automated business systems. They must understand the capabilities of present-day technology and must be able to identify where technology can increase productivity and provide opportunities to reduce cost and expand their market. The subsidiaries must understand and accept the need for structured methods of systems design and development and must appreciate the need for standards and consistent methodologies. They must participate in quality control and project management and must also be receptive to new ideas and techniques.

During this period, the users will be able to perform an increasing number of tasks previously requiring the capabilities of a computer programmer. More and more report writers and special user-oriented utility programs will become available. The programmer will emphasize construction of data bases and their maintenance. The end users will also be increasingly able to develop their own data collection schemes.

The Corporation: Management will become increasingly dependent on the generation of internal information for automated systems whose cost will continue to grow. Nevertheless, the potential for increasing productivity and management effectiveness is enormous. The reliability and security of these systems will be critical.

Corporate officers must play an active role in the selection and evaluation of these systems. They must set the priorities and approve the expenditures. They must be familiar with both the needs of the corporation and the available technology. They must require justification for projects and support the development and enforcement of standards.

SUBSIDIARY ANALYSIS

Introduction

Key individuals from every ABC subsidiary were interviewed by utilizing a technique called WOTS-UP analysis, which provides insight into the organization's:

- Weaknesses – those qualities lacking in the organization primarily relating to data processing
- Opportunities – programs that, if implemented, could provide significant improvements
- Threats – occurrences that could severely affect the profitability of the organization and could even put it out of business
- Strengths – opposite of weaknesses

In the following sections, the WOTS-UP analysis for each subsidiary is documented and accompanied by a set of long-term and short-term programs.

ABC MOVING AND STORAGE

Mission Statement

ABC provides local and intrastate transportation and storage of household goods, business records, and electronic equipment through local branch offices. The trend is to mechanize the branch office activities and integrate them with the central operation.

Weaknesses

- Field management data processing knowledge is limited
- Standardization of operations and training of field personnel is an ongoing activity because of high staff turnover
- Centralized systems are integrated with field systems
- The record storage system has serious flaws

Strengths

- Pursuit of nonregulated business opportunities
- Desire to reduce work flows and automate processes
- Good data processing knowledge of the upper-level managers at the central facility
- A new breed of branch management that is energetic and well educated

Threats

- Loss of the central computer, which would affect profitability and long-range strategic plans
- Misplaced business records
- Unauthorized access to computerized customer information

Opportunities

- Expansion of information systems reporting to provide greater central office control and responsive management
- Development of a single revenue document for the field that would be input to several computerized applications
- Expansion of the branch office computer application to include management reports on daily sales, a decentralized storage system, record storage data entry, truck dispatching, vehicle maintenance, word processing, and connection to the host computer
- Upgrading of branch office telephone systems as required

MIS Goals

MIS must continue to meet the growing information and automation needs of ABC Moving and Storage. By providing systems analysis support, MIS can assist in the streamlining of paper flow. The branch office and central site computers will be used together to provide workable solutions.

Plans and Programs

- Continue installation of the branch office computer system
- Evaluate the potential for additional automation of the branch offices Implement those systems that have high benefit and broad application
- Redesign the field revenue document and supporting systems. This endeavor will require interfacing with a salesman commission system, the general ledger system, and the accounts receivable system
- Redesign the storage system and implement user data entry at the central location

ABC Moving and Storage 1983 MIS Project List

1. Do systems maintenance
2. Complete the installation of branch office computers
3. Enhance the branch office system with new applications including: revenue document processing, weekly management report, and word processing
4. Develop a revenue accounting system
5. Support timesharing usage
6. Install a new release of the general ledger
7. Bring accounts payable, accounts receivable, and general ledger online
8. Redesign the claims reporting system

2
Operational Planning and Budgeting

After the MIS manager develops the strategic plan utilizing the WOTS-UP analysis, the next step should be the development of the operational plans and budgets. This chapter discusses the annual planning and budgeting cycle and introduces the *zero base budgeting* (ZBB) methodology. The first part of the chapter discusses the differences and relationships between strategic planning and operational planning. The second part introduces an integrated annual budgeting system that incorporates flexible budgeting, zero base budgeting, participative budgeting, management by objectives (MBO), responsibility accounting, and feedback information. The next focus is on ZBB, its definition, and how it differs from traditional incremental budgeting. Fourth, industrial and governmental applications of ZBB are summarized. The fifth part discusses ZBB strengths and weaknesses and the sixth part describes the ZBB procedure. Finally, a presentation of the conditions necessary for a successful application of zero base budgeting is made.

OPERATIONAL PLANNING VERSUS STRATEGIC PLANNING

The operational plan is generally equivalent to the MIS annual project plan. It provides a one year set of objectives and detailed budget preparation, manpower scheduling, and timetables for individual projects. For data processing, operational planning involves understanding what kinds of hardware, software, and personnel will be needed in the coming year together with their associated costs. Figures 2.1, 2.2, and 2.3 present examples of hardware, software, and DP personnel requirement schedules.

The strategic and operational plans differ in more ways than the number of years covered. First, the strategic plan tends to be more general because of the greater number of unknowns associated with the long term. Planned cost estimates are rougher in the strategic

SAMPLE HARDWARE REQUIREMENTS PLAN 1983				
Computer Memory				1 Megabyte
Disk Storage	2 Spindles			
Tape Storage			1 Drive & Cntlr	
CRTs	4 Order Entry	2 Finance	2 Billing	3 EDP
Additional Lease Cost per Month	$1,400	$200	$800	$3,300
	Jan-Mar	Apr-Jun	Jul-Sep	Oct-Dec

Figure 2.1. Sample Hardware Requirements Plan 1983

SAMPLE SOFTWARE REQUIREMENTS PLAN 1983				
Data Base	DB language	DB dictionary		
Financial Model				Autotab
Performance Monitors			Disk file monitor	
Billing System				Report Generator
Additional Lease Cost per Month	$400	$200	$200	$20,500 (once)
	Jan-Mar	Apr-Jun	Jul-Sep	Oct-Dec

Figure 2.2. Sample Software Requirements Plan 1983

plan than in the operational plan. The strategic plan outlines what MIS can and *should do* for each department (or division); the operational plan itemizes what MIS *will do* in the coming year. Operational planning is essential if MIS is to anticipate the company's needs and have them reflected in annual budgets.

The primary input to the operational plan is the strategic plan. Portions of the Plans and Programs section of the strategic plan (see

SAMPLE PERSONNEL REQUIREMENTS PLAN 1983				
Data Base Manager	1 @ $35K			
Analysts			1 @ $30K	
Programmers	2 @ $25K			1 @ $25K
Data Entry	2 @ $10K	1 @ $10K		2 @ $10K
Education Expense	$1,000	$200	$500	$800
	Jan-Mar	Apr-Jun	Jul-Sep	Oct-Dec

Figure 2.3. Sample Personnel Requirements Plan 1983

Chapter 1) should comprise the majority of the operational plan supplemented by activities of an on-going nature such as maintenance. Figure 2.4 illustrates the relationship between strategic planning and operational planning and budgeting (Lin 1979). Planning includes nonquantitative goals whereas budgeting deals only with quantitative financial goals. Planning usually provides a general guide or direction to operations; budgeting is primarily a control for specific activities. The overall process of strategic planning, operational planning, and budgeting starts with setting goals, objectives, and strategies.

The goal is a statement of the guiding philosophy and is not quantified. A goal for MIS could be: to provide cost-effective data processing services of high quality while providing for future needs and minimizing operating costs. Objectives are specific, quantified statements tied to the basic goal. Examples of MIS objectives include reducing the frequency of late report deliveries from 10 to 5%, limiting the MIS chargeout rate to last year's level despite inflation, and improving the uptime of the data communications network from 95 to 98%. The strategies indicate how the MIS manager will obtain the desired goals and objectives. Strategies used in this sense refer to action plans and are not to be confused with the strategic planning process.

Every year the MIS manager must review the strategic plans to consider past performance and external environmental changes and make specific decisions as to the implementation of strategies, projects, and operational plans. Key elements in an MIS budget include salaries and personnel expenses, hardware expenses, office

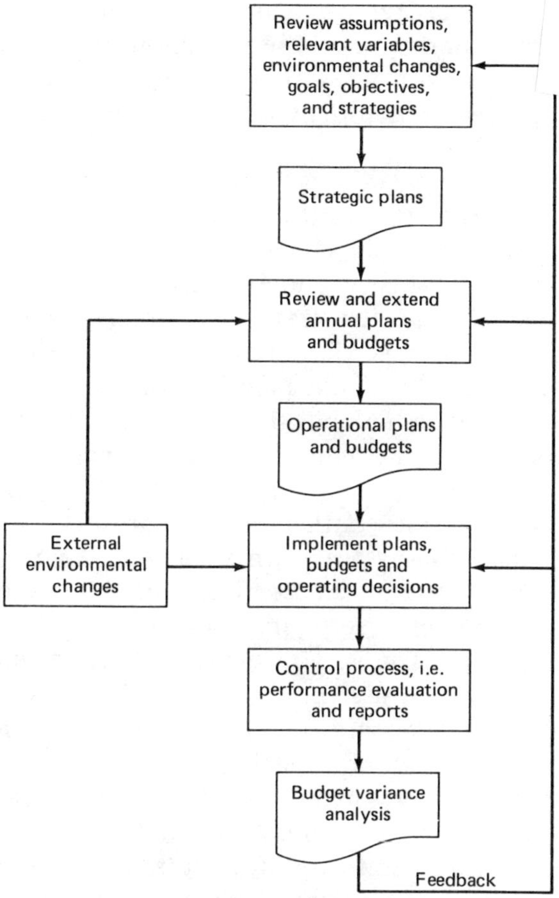

Figure 2.4. Strategic planning, operational planning, and the budgeting process (Adapted from Lin 1979, p. 30).

equipment, software purchases and maintenance, supplies, telecommunication expenses, office space, electricity, and other expenses such as travel, education, office supplies, insurance, and so forth. A more detailed explanation of the various types of expenditures is contained in Chapter 5.

Implementation of plans and budgets starts with their distribution to key personnel and the conducting of relevant conferences to communicate with and educate people. It ends with the execution of plans, budgets, and operating decisions. The control process includes measuring performance, reporting and results, analyzing budget variances, considering alternative courses of action, and choosing the best action, as well as follow-up action and feedback to the planning process. This process is pictorially represented in Figure 2.4.

AN INTEGRATED ANNUAL BUDGETING SYSTEM

How does the MIS manager choose those projects that should be included in the schedule for next year? The real answer is that he does not. The MIS manager has no authority to set the direction of the entire company. He cannot be expected to know, for example, that the controller has as an objective the automation of the accounts receivable function and he will suffer some bonus time if MIS "fails again."

The solution to these conflicts over priorities is to let the user department management set its own priorities. If you provide a list of all possible projects with an assessment of the resources required for each, the various managers can rationally choose which projects will get worked on. That is, you manage a service function with a charter to serve the end user needs. Let them decide what projects to be worked on. That is not to say that you cannot lobby for the projects you want, however. Just let them make the major project selection decisions. If the marketing vice president does not participate and speak up early, let him be silent for the rest of the year. But how do you organize this priority setting process in an orderly manner that will encourage user management participation. The first step is to assess each activity using zero base budgeting in the quantification process and a user management committee in the priority-setting process. The remainder of this chapter and Chapters 3 and 4 describe how ZBB has been successfully applied to MIS activities.

The zero base budgeting system is a subset of the overall company budgeting system. Figure 2.5 presents an overall budgeting system which is an integration of flexible budgeting, participative budgeting, management by objectives, responsibility accounting, and feedback information. (This section is adapted from Lin 1979.)

The budget system starts with a goal-setting process. A concurrent process of flexible budgeting also takes place. In contrast to fixed budgeting, flexible budgeting is a control technique to aid manage-

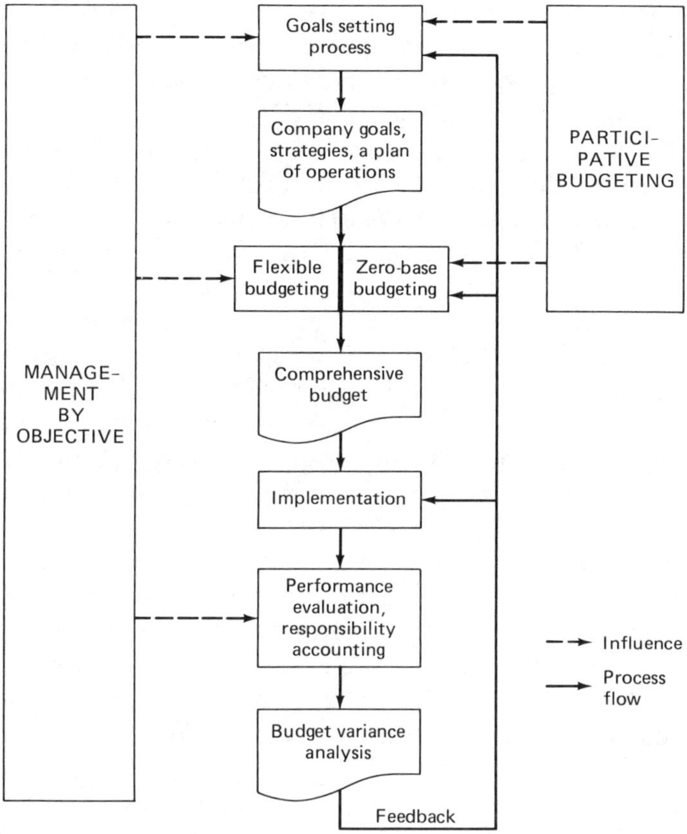

Figure 2.5. An integrated budgeting system (Adapted from Lin 1979, p. 32).

ment in adjusting to a changing environment by providing an adjustable budget that is related to production or sales volume. Zero base budgeting is a method of reevaluating all programs and expenditures every year. The process requires each manager to justify his entire budget request in detail and puts the burden of proof on him to justify why he should spend any money. Zero base budgeting requires that each activity be described in terms of "decision packages." Each decision package must contain information concerning an activity's purposes, the consequences of not performing the activity, measures of performance, alternative courses of action, and the costs and benefits of the activity. It should focus both on various ways of performing a given activity and alternative levels of effort of performing it. The three basic steps of zero base budgeting are (1) developing decision packages, (2) ranking packages in order of importance through cost-benefit analysis or subjective evaluation, and (3) allocating resources accordingly.

Flexible budgeting will be used by managers of departments related to production and sales. Such flexible budgets would provide data on expenses that make it possible to compute budget allowances for various volumes or rates of activity in each department. Zero base budgeting will apply to manufacturing services and support areas as well as department and corporate overhead. Participative budgeting is applied at all levels of management. The suggestions and competence of management are taken seriously and have a significant impact. Top management must become deeply involved in developing broad objectives, strategies, and goals. All participating managers must be committed to implement their agreed-upon goals and budgeted figures.

A traditional accounting system should be modified to have responsibility accounting based on activities or programs. Monthly performance reports should conform to the responsibility centers and should emphasize controllable items only. Depreciation and corporate allocations may be charged to the manager's department but should not be included in the evaluation of that manager's performance.

Feedback information is the key to continued success. In order to know whether or not progress is being made, the manager must have complete feedback in a form that can be understood.

Management by objectives is the fundamental activity in the integrated budgeting system (see Figure 2.5). At the outset, it is important that the mechanism for a free flow of information leading to the development of commonly understood corporate goals and strategies be installed and working. Management by objectives is the means by which all levels of management, through exchanges of information relevant to corporate and department goals, obtain agreement and understanding about what the company and the department are attempting to accomplish.

In summary, the integrated budgeting system should involve the construction and maintenance of company and departmental goals through management by objectives. By formalizing the MBOs, the company establishes a basis for participative budgeting, as represented in the flexible budgeting and the zero base budgeting processes, and provides a basis for a responsibility-accounting reporting feedback system that allows the users of resources to take corrective action or make adjustments to meet company and departmental goals.

AN OVERVIEW OF ZBB

Peter A. Pyhrr has defined zero base budgeting as:

> An operating, planning and budgeting process which requires each manager to justify his entire budget request in detail from scratch (hence zero base) and shifts the burden of proof to each manager to justify why he should spend any money at all. This approach requires that all activities be defined in 'decision packages' which will be evaluated by systematic analysis and ranked in order of importance. (Pyhrr 1972)

The develop of ZBB goes back to 1964 when it was introduced in the United States Department of Agriculture. Then, in 1969 while at Texas Instruments, Peter Pyhrr further developed the concept. Texas Instruments first used it in its staff and research divisions and then expanded its use to the entire company in the following year. ZBB is a general management tool that companies and institutions can use to improve planning, budgeting, and operational decision making. The underlying concept is systemization of the companies' and institutions' operational planning and budgeting processes. ZBB is applicable in both the private and public sectors and has even been recommended for personal applications.

ZBB is different from the traditional incremental budgeting approach. The traditional (incremental) budget assumes that budgeted expenses for the coming year will be no less than the preceeding year's budget or some average of preceeding years. There are three major problems with traditional incremental budgeting approaches. First, since managers know their initial budget requests will be slashed due to limited total available funds, they usually inflate them by building in additional slack. Second, since it is difficult to translate long-term objectives into action plans and budgets, the new projects, no matter how important, are often the first items cut from the budget when funding requests exceed available funds. Finally, the key problems and decision areas are not always highlighted and trade-offs among long-term objectives and programs, operating needs, and profits are not clearly identified. Zero base budgeting attempts to reevaluate all programs, activities, and expenditures in terms of cost-benefit. It is not based on last year's budget but rather on "ground zero." That is, it is predicated on the belief that some obsolete programs should be eliminated. It is a method of forcing managers to justify every controllable activity.

With zero base budgeting and starting at an organization's lowest-level cost centers, managers must justify everything they do, both old and new, as if they were building their operation from scratch. The process of ZBB focuses on the creation and evaluation of "decision packages." A decision package is a document that identifies and describes a specific activity in such a manner that management can (1) evaluate it and rank it against other activities competing for limited resources and (2) decide whether to approve or disapprove it. Each manager prepares decision packages for the operations he controls and ranks all of them by priority. The manager then passes this ranking on to his superior who goes through the same exercise at a higher level. It essentially is a priority ranking of endorsed projects by the lowest management level followed by a hierarchical review with continual consolidated reranking. This process will not necessarily ensure that an item included in last year's budget will reappear in this year's budget.

In traditional budgeting, a company makes budget decisions first which then become a rigid framework within which line managers must make their operating plans. Additionally, from an analysis of decision packages in ZBB, management gets not only a budget but also an operational plan. Under ZBB the budget is a product of the operating decisions. Hence, ZBB appears to be a more flexible tool in the budgeting process. Figure 2.6 is a summary of a comparison between traditional budgeting and ZBB (Phyrr 1976). As shown, both start from some form of strategic planning during which objectives, goals, strategies, and major programs are defined. During the operational planning and budgeting stage, both processes develop sales forecasts and direct costs of materials, labor, and overhead.

During this stage of the budget process, traditional and ZBB methods differ. Under traditional budgeting, management first estimates the discretionary costs of current activities. This estimate

Planning/Budgeting Sequence	Traditional	Zero Base
1. Strategic planning (2–5 years)	Establish goals, objectives, and strategies	Establish goals, objectives, and strategies
2. Operational planning and budgeting (1 year)	Develop sales forecast	Develop sales forecast
	Establish cost budgets for direct labor, materials and overhead	Establish cost budgets for direct labor, materials, and overhead
	Estimate discretionary costs of current activities	Evaluate current nonproduction activities and alternatives
	Estimate costs of new activities	Identify and evaluate new activities and alternatives
	Develop detailed budgets	Establish priorities
3. Evaluation and review of budget	Test budget amount against objectives	Test budget against plan
		Establish tradeoffs among current operations, develop needs and profits
4. Final budget	Final budget	Establish budget and operational plan
		Develop detailed budgets

Figure 2.6. Traditional versus zero-base budgeting. Reprinted, by permission of the publisher, from "Zero-Base Budgeting: Where to Use It and How to Begin," Peter A. Pyhrr, p. 11 of *S.A.M. Advanced Management Journal,* Summer, 1976, © 1976 by the Society for Advancement of Management, a Division of American Management Associations, New York. All rights reserved.

serves as the base for the budget of the upcoming year. New activities are considered, and those chosen will be funded. These detailed budgets are then submitted to top management for review and approval. If rejected, the budget is sent back down the ranks for revision.

Under the ZBB process, current activities and alternatives are evaluated together with the new programs. Operating managers establish their priorities and thereby identify the tradeoffs between expenditure levels and operating needs. New activities can be ranked higher than current ones and, thus, new programs can be funded with existing funding levels.

Using ZBB, top management can readily test the budget against the operational plan since they are looking at an evaluation in terms of priorities rather than in terms of numbers. From its analysis of the decision packages, management gets not only a budget but an operational plan by which to test the budget.

Zero base budgeting can highlight long-run strategic problems, for example, development funds that are not adequate for planned future growth or marketing support that is not sufficient to achieve budgeted sales volume. Because of its impact on all planning elements, ZBB forces management to make different trade-offs among current operations, development needs, and profits. Once the budgets have been approved, the detailed budgeting and fine tuning of numbers can be done.

ZBB does not supplement the entire corporate budget. It is not suited to all organizations or to all types of activities of an organization. It has little use in budgeting for production costs such as direct labor, direct materials, and direct overhead which are largely determined by production and sales volume. It is primarily applicable to the service and support areas of an organization which have discretionary costs. Typical examples of activities that can be assisted by ZBB are maintenance, supervision, production planning, industrial engineering, quality control, data processing, advertising, accounting, training, personnel, tax, and legal activities. Within MIS, the development area is obviously the most appropriate for application of zero base budgeting but ZBB will provide significant benefits when applied to the entire MIS organization.

ZBB is not a total management system nor a management process. It will not correct bad planning or poor execution. It is not a total replacement for any familiar budgeting process, but it supplements and strengthens planning and budgeting systems. It does not stand alone. The organization needs an effective overall planning and budgeting system which ZBB supplements. There is a need for cooperation from all levels of management: the operational manager, general managers, and top management. The contributions of top management include overall organizational goals, operating strategy assumptions, and policy guidelines while lower managers must prepare decision packages because pertinent detailed information is more readily available at the lower levels. Each level of management must take the ranking process seriously if a relevant set of activities listed in order of priority is to be achieved.

INDUSTRIAL AND GOVERNMENTAL APPLICATIONS OF ZBB

The majority of recent applications of ZBB in the private sector have been modeled after the initial venture at Texas Instruments in 1969.

The process was first implemented within Texas Instruments' research and development (R and D) department. Decision packages were designed to specify the objectives of R and D activities and to describe the benefits, costs, alternatives, and consequences of not funding each R and D program. The research and development programs were then ranked according to potential benefits, and limited funds were allocated to those programs with the highest priority.

In 1971, the management at Texas Instruments decided to use the new technique in other nonproduction and staff areas within the company. In the next year, ZBB became the standard operating procedure for all staff and research activities, which consists of over one-third of the company's annual budget.

Several surveys of ZBB's usefulness were made in 1976 and 1977. Stonich (1977) obtained information from 54 companies that had implemented ZBB prior to 1976. He asked ZBB users to estimate how much their operating budgets had changed as a result of using ZBB. Thirteen percent reported a decrease of more than 10%, 30% reported a budget decrease of between 5 and 10%, 51% said that their budgets had changed (increased or decreased) less than 5%, and 7% of the respondents reported a budget increase of more than 5%.

Respondents were also asked for their overall evaluation of ZBB as a management planning and control system. Twenty-eight percent gave an "excellent" rating, 59% rated ZBB "good," and 13% gave only a "fair" rating. None listed ZBB as "poor."

The American Management Association commissioned a study by Austin (1977) to explore the organizational impact and effects of ZBB. Of the 223 companies responding to the survey, 57 indicated they are using ZBB, 33 are in the planning and implementation stages, and 5 companies terminated the use of ZBB. In general, the responses show that included in the positive results of ZBB implementation are better resource allocation, improved decision making, facilitation of planning, and reduction in costs and personnel. However, 70% stated it had little or no impact on resource allocation and 47% mentioned that the effect of ZBB on profitability was of little or no value. Future surveys might attempt to measure the relative successes or failures of the decision unit managers. A report of fewer ulcers and higher bonuses has more meaning to these individuals and would definitely give them more incentive.

Dean (1977), in a survey of 15 large companies, identified eight important reasons for using zero base budgeting: (1) ZBB considers alternative ways of performing the same job, (2) it focuses the management process on analysis and decision making, (3) it improves the planning process, (4) it requires each budget request to be justified, (5) it permits trade-offs within and/or across departments, (6) it relates program costs to benefits, (7) it enables top management to follow up on cost and performance, and (8) it reduces duplication of staff efforts. Dean also recognized six problems that ZBB users encounter: (1) difficulty in evaluating different or dissimilar functional decision packages on the same scale, (2) more time and effort required, (3) difficulty in ranking a large number of decision packages, (4) increased administrative and communication efforts, (5) managers' feeling of being threatened by ZBB, and (6) unavailability or difficulty of obtaining required cost/performance information.

The Chicago office of Peat, Marwick, Mitchell and Company (1977a) also conducted a survey of 391 business executives and government officials. The results showed that 81% of the responses indicated that "certain aspects of Zero Base Budgeting would improve our present budgeting procedures," and 47% stated that "we are likely to seriously consider implementation of a revised budgeting system using the ZBB approach or elements of it." Tourangeau (1979), reporting on Canadian applications of ZBB, revealed that 60% of the 333 organizations surveyed are using or are seriously considering using ZBB.

In summary, ZBB has been adopted in many U.S. and Canadian companies with an overall measure of success. This budgeting tool offers a means of objectively allocating funds to obtain maximum benefit in nonproduction departments. However, the demands of additional time and paperwork are not acceptable in many firms. It would be beneficial to obtain additional feedback from those companies that have tried the technique and subsequently cast it aside as impractical. This information would give added insights into the usefulness of ZBB.

Georgia was the first state government to adopt ZBB for the fiscal year 1972–1973. In his budget address to the joint session of the General Assembly of Georgia on January 13, 1972, Governor Jimmy Carter credited the early implementation of his reorganization study and the new zero base budget for cutting the spending plans for the current year by $55 million with no significant decrease in state services. The Georgia ZBB system had the full support of Governor

Carter, as evidenced by his statement in an interview conducted on January 7, 1974: "I think our Zero Base Budgeting system is great for management's decision-making . . . . Because of Zero Base Budgeting, we were able to determine that seven different agencies had the responsibility for the education of deaf children. When we broke down the 11,000 or so decision packages and put a computer number on each kind of function, those functions were very quickly identified as being duplicated" (Carter 1974).

Hermanson and Minmier (1976) conducted a survey of all of Georgia's 13 department heads and 39 budgeting analysts. Their study showed that Mr. Carter's strong support of the ZBB system was not shared by some of the department heads. For example, of the 13 department heads interviewed during this survey, only 2 indicated strong support for the zero base budgeting system. The other department heads expressed varying degrees of dissatisfaction with this new budgeting system. The study also showed that (1) 53% of the total respondents believed that the advanced planning was inadequate, (2) 68% indicated an improvement in the quality of management information, (3) only 7% perceived some shifting of financial resources as a result of the use of the new system, (4) 62.5% believed that it was not practical to prepare a decision package representing a minimum level of effort, and (5) 84% recommended the continued use of zero base budgeting in some form.

Peat, Marwick, Mitchell and Company (1977b) undertook a limited survey of federal officials in 10 agencies questioning them about their expectations regarding ZBB and about any actions they had taken to prepare for it. The results showed that most agencies and departments believed they could proceed with budget preparation using the ZBB approach immediately, if so required. However, 50% of the agencies said that guidance on procedural matters would be necessary from the Office of Management and Budget. They also stated that top management support would be necessary for the successful implementation of zero base budgeting.

Schick and Keith (1977) reported that ZBB is used by 11 state governments. In 1974 Garland, Texas, was the first municipality to use it. A study by Scott (1977) has indicated that approximately two dozen cities use ZBB. Zero base budgeting was mandated in the federal government by former President Carter soon after he was inaugurated in January, 1977. The ZBB process was introduced in all executive departments and agencies in 1977 for preparation of the federal government's budget for fiscal year 1979. It was abandonded by President Reagan in the Summer of 1981.

STRENGTHS AND WEAKNESSES OF ZBB

There are many benefits of using zero base budgeting:

1. The primary benefit derived from the use of ZBB is a systematic method of evaluating the nonproduction activities of an organization. If properly implemented, the technique provides a rational means of reducing or expanding the proposed budget and encourages the allocation of resources from low- to high-priority activities.
2. Closely related to the concept of management by objectives, ZBB allows greater participation in the budgeting process by lower-level management. They are given the opportunity to choose which alternative is most effective in accomplishing stated objectives and have a better understanding of the specific costs and benefits of their activities. As with the use of MBO, greater participation can often lead to increased commitment.
3. Outdated programs that have outlived their usefulness can be identified and changed. This is significant in a changing operating environment where available resources are scarce.
4. To achieve greater flexibility in the budgeting process, ZBB can be effectively used in conjunction with the technique of variable budgeting. Variable budgeting can provide more meaningful information during budgeting of production-related activities whereas ZBB can improve decision making for nonproduction functions. In addition, ZBB can make variable budgeting more effective by periodically reevaluating the proper levels of manufacturing overhead applied in variable budgets.

There are four major weaknesses in apply ZBB:

1. The most widely cited argument against ZBB is the additional time required for the technique. These time demands are at

their height in the first year of implementation when the budgeting tool receives its most critical evaluation. Pyhrr asserts that with experience, ZBB actually decreases time spent in budgeting, but this has yet to be conclusively demonstrated.

2. In conjunction with increased time demands, paperwork is also greatly expanded with ZBB. The extra burden of handling thousands of individual decision packages is considered unfeasible in many budgeting departments. In Georgia, the use of ZBB created 11,000 decision packages. To many, the cost of acquiring all this information is not justified by the benefits obtained.
3. The structure of public sector organizations put additional constraints on the use of ZBB. Political pressure to maintain the status quo and, particularly, constraints against personnel cutbacks are excessive. Added to this pressure is a fear of putting too much budgetary power in the hands of the chief executive.
4. Some accuse the title *zero base budgeting* of being an illusion. When the technique is actually used, budgets are not scrutinized to a zero level but only down to from 60 to 80% of current budget funding. This argument seems to be a semantic difference of opinion since the levels of examination can be flexibly applied in each organization.

THE ZERO BASE BUDGETING PROCEDURE

Cheek (1977) presented the six-step ZBB procedure as shown in Figure 2.7.

1. *Defining the objectives.* The first step of the ZBB procedure is to establish objectives for the effort. An objective could be simply to prepare an MIS operating budget, to reduce overall MIS budget costs by 5%, or both. MIS objectives have to be tied to overall company objectives. The specific quantitative objectives for the upcoming year should be based on sound economic assumptions. For example, the lower-level manager makes assumptions about inflation rates and salary increases and needs information about service-level requirements for other related departments. At this stage the MIS department will receive the following documents from headquarters:

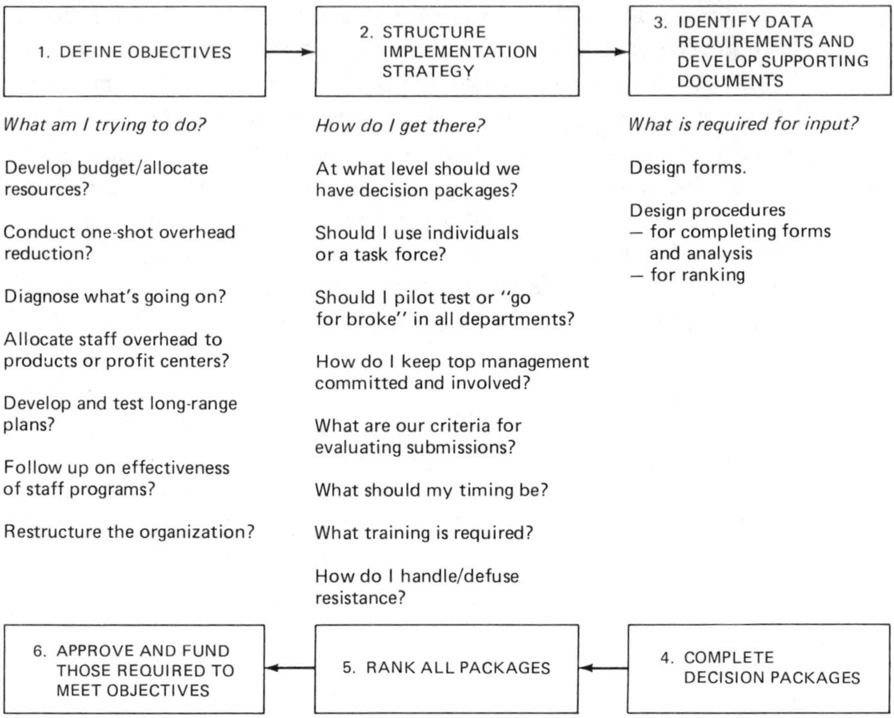

Figure 2.7. Sequence of steps for designing and implementing a zero-base budgeting system. Reprinted, by permission of the publisher, from Zero-Base Budgeting Comes of Age by Logan M. Cheek, p. 20, © 1977 by AMACOM, a division of American Management Associations, New York. All rights reserved.

a. A letter of transmittal from the chief executive regarding the upcoming operational plan and ZBB.
b. A discussion of the purpose, objectives, and basic concepts of ZBB.
c. An economic overview of the firm and its industry as an introduction to the firm's goals, objectives, planning assumptions, and spending guidelines.

2. *Structuring the implementation strategy*. After defining the objectives, the next step is to determine how to achieve them. The questions to be answered include: What are our decision units going to be? Who will be responsible for implementing ZBB? What role will top management play? What kind of training is necessary? What schedule would provide adequate time to do a high-quality job? Can the computer help streamline the process?

A decision unit is usually defined as a basic activity or group of activities that management considers for planning, analysis, and review. In other words, a decision unit is generally the lowest-level of activity about which budget decisions are made. Considerations such as the size of the organization, the range of activities, and the availability of accounting and workload data should dictate the size and extent of the decision unit. Examples include a special work assignment, major projects, capital projects, services received or provided, line item of expenditure, specific MIS functions, and so forth.

Stonich (1977) suggested that it is desirable for decision units to be roughly similar in size in terms of both personnel and dollars. Proper analysis cannot be performed on very large decision units because they tend to include a multiplicity of activities which complicates the incremental analysis that takes place later. A unit that is too small is not easily analyzed because it is difficult to develop practical lower or higher levels of service. Also, if units are very small, so large a number of them are identified that the total analysis is unwieldy. He suggested that typical decision units should include between 5 and 15 people and a dollar budget of about $150,000 to $400,000 on a full-cost basis.

All levels of managers are responsible for implementing ZBB. Top management should play an active role in the ZBB process. For MIS activities, three criteria should be used for stating anticipated benefits: (1) improved user service, (2) more efficient processing, and (3) reduced cost. The amount of time required to establish and implement both traditional budgeting and ZBB are about the same. It takes about from three to six months for a relatively uncomplicated ZBB process, longer for very large companies. Training of departmental personnel is another important task. Training should start with an orientation seminar for department heads. This can be a three hour department meeting to present the purpose, concepts, and principles of ZBB and to emphasize the value of departmental goals, objectives, and workload measures. The next step is to train people for their role in the formulation of decision units, packages, and ranking. Training should be provided for all levels of management.

3. *Developing the supporting system.* The supporting system for ZBB consists of the following documents: decision package forms with worksheets if desired, ranking forms, and a procedures manual. Decision package forms and ranking forms will be discussed in more detail in Chapter 3 and 4. Cheek (1977) suggested the following contents for a ZBB procedures manual:
   a. A letter of transmittal from top management
   b. A statement of the purpose and objectives of ZBB
   c. An economic overview of the firm and its industry
   d. The procedure for preparing decision packages
   e. The procedure for ranking decision packages
   f. A detailed implementation schedule.

   Figure 2.8 presents an example of a detailed implementation schedule adapted from Cheek (1977).
4. *Preparing the decision packages.* The fourth step is to describe each activity with a decision package. The decision package, the building block of the ZBB concept, is a document that identifies and describes each decision unit in such a manner that management can evaluate it, rank it against other units, and decide whether to approve or disapprove the funding. The lowest-level manager responsible for the decision unit prepares the package. *The decision package usually includes:* (1) objective, purpose, and scope, (2) what is to be done and how, (3) consequences of not doing the activity, (4) alternative methods, (5) alternative levels, (6) costs and benefits of recommended alternative methods and levels, and (7) resources required.

   In preparing decision packages, a decision unit manager begins with the specification of the activity's objective and purpose. Then he should describe how the activity currently is handled and the resources utilized. Next, he developes workload and performance measurement techniques, considers alternative methods of operating, and makes an incremental analysis. The final decision package will be placed in one of the following three categories: (1) different methods and/or levels of effort to do each activity, (2) "business as usual" levels of effort where there are no other alternatives,

1978–1979 Zero Base Budget Calendar

Task	*Prime Mover(s)*	*Due Date*	*Audience*
1. Set up procedures and forms.	Budget Staff	Done	
2. Kick off process and conduct training sessions.	CEO Budget Staff	6/1–6/14	H. Q. Managers
3. Recast 1977 budget into decision packages for "live" ranking.	H. Q. Managers	6/15–7/6	Budget Staff/ Managers
4. Critique process and conduct checkpoint with executive committee.	Budget Staff	7/7–7/14	Exec. Comm.
5. Develop 1978–1979 budget and rank at section level.	H. Q. Managers	7/14–8/4	Dept. Heads
6. Review and conduct initial ranking at department level.	Dept. Heads	8/4–8/11	Staff VPs
7. Refine packages and conduct final ranking.	Dept. Heads	8/11–8/18	Staff VPs
8. Present findings and recommended 1978–1979 budget.	Staff VPs	8/18–9/1	Exec. Comm.
9. Approve final budget.	CEO Exec. Comm.	9/1–9/8	–
10. Consolidate submissions for control.	Budget Staff	9/8–9/22	VP Finance
11. Critique process with staff managers and department heads.	Budget Staff	9/22–10/6	Dept. Heads/ Staff Managers
12. Conduct checkpoint review on system, refine approach for 1979–1980.	Controller	10/6–10/13	Exec. Comm.
13. Implement recommended changes.	Budget Staff	Open	–

Figure 2.8. A sample ZBB implementation schedule. Reprinted, by permission of the publisher, from Zero-Base Budgeting Comes of Age by Logan M. Cheek, p. 189, © 1977 by AMACOM, a division of American Management Associations, New York. All rights reserved.

or the present method and level of effort is required, and (3) new activities and programs. An example of a decision package for a computer audit department is shown in Figure 2.9. Identifying additional levels of effort is an important aspect of ZBB. If only one level of effort is analyzed (probably reflecting the funding level desired by the manager) and the

Francl, Lin and Vasarhelyi
Certified Public Accountants

Decision Package

Activity name:	*Computer Audit Department*		
Director/manager:	*Gliesman*	Date:	*07/01/82*
Effort level:	*1 of 3*	Rank:	*6*
This level is:	*Equal to the current level of effort.*		

DESCRIPTION OF ACTIVITY

This activity provides assistance to the general audit function by reviewing and evaluating EDP controls as associated with accounting applications of the firm's auditing clients.

OBJECTIVES OR ACTIVITY

To satisfy generally accepted auditing procedures as outlined by the various prounouncements governed by the AICPA. This will allow us to ensure ourselves of the validity of accounting data at the processing level rather than to rely on generated reports by the client.

MEASURES OF PERFORMANCE

Direct measures include: a decrease in year-end validation work based on increased reliance on computer application control, increased coverage of client data through computer assisted auditing techniques, and reduction in client fees due to reduction in outside consultation thus allowing us a better market position.

BENEFITS FROM FUNDING

Along with the procedural benefits, this activity will allow us to maintain our present market share as our client's growth and sophistication increases. It is estimated that employing outside firms to perform reviews would cost $75,000 annually. Having an in-house EDP specialist would create a more cohesive and overall effective approach for out audit effort.

CONSEQUENCES OF NOT FUNDING

Besides the loss of benefits as described above, there will be an increase in the probability of not being in compliance with generally accepted auditing procedures, increased costs due to uncontrolled factors in outside consulting services (i.e., scheduling), and limitations for growth potential for our office.

PROJECTED REVENUES AND/OR COSTS

Annual salary – EDP Specialist	$35,000
Clerical staff:	12,000
Other costs:	5,000
Total projected costs	$52,000

Costs include an EDP Audit Specialist, one clerical person, and specific costs attributable to this function. All other costs associated with the normal auditing function is contained in the General Audit Practice, Decision Package No. 13.

Figure 2.9.

ALTERNATIVE APPROACHES

1. Use outside CPA consulting services.
2. Restrict engagements to clients maintaining simple EDP applications or none at all.

Both of the above are considered inferior based upon the growth potential of this office of the firm.

Figure 2.9. Continued.

request from the manager for funds exceeds funding availability, management has no choice but to do one of four things: fund the activity at the requested level, which reduces profits; eliminate it, make arbitrary reductions; or recycle the budgetary process. However, with ZBB, by stating the various levels of effort, recycling the budget process is avoided because top management will already possess alternative levels of effort to choose from. A decision package can be thought of as one incremental level in a decision unit, though there may be several decision packages for each activity. It is these incremental levels that get ranked.

While only minimal data is required to complete an activity description, each company will want to tailor the decision packages to its own needs. The validation of accuracy is made by balancing existing activities against the current budget. The MIS manager should be aware of the tendency to pad the manpower estimates.

5. *Ranking all decision packages.* Once the manager has defined all his obligatory and discretionary activities into packages, a ranking process occurs. Usually the manager ranks all packages in order of their decreasing benefit to the company on a cost/benefit basis. This ranking activity begins at the cost-center level. A committee formed by all managers in the MIS department then reviews all the packages presented to it and ranks them in order of importance by means of a voting mechanism. The packages that are considered most beneficial to the cost center as a whole receive the highest rankings, whereas the least important receive the lowest. A cutoff point is now established. Given the general level of funds that are available in the coming fiscal year, all packages above a

given ranking are accepted by the group and all those below a certain point are rejected.

These decisions are then passed up to the next higher management level where the manager reviews the rankings to determine if they fit into the organization's goals and decides whether the rejected packages offer enough benefits to expand the level of funding. Upper managers briefly examine only a preestablished percentage of the packages so as to control their time involvement. This process is repeated until all the accepted activities are filtered through to the top of the organization where the budget for the entire organization is then created.

6. *Approving the selected decision packages.* Once the ranking decisions have been made, funding allocation decisions are made and detailed budgets are prepared. Managers will know both the budget amount and output performance measures. The ZBB documents that are returned to the decision units become a reference plan that managers can use for controlling their activities during the operating year.

GUIDELINES FOR SUCCESSFUL ZBB IMPLEMENTATION

Many of the companies adopting the ZBB process believe that the benefits outweigh the costs of increased time and effort. The benefits include a greater understanding of how funds are being used, increased participation by lower management in budgeting, and the elimination of inefficient programs. However, because the budgeting tool involves the costs of increased time, paperwork, and effort, the implementation decision must be carefully considered.

ZBB is not and should not be considered a panacea for management's budgeting problems. ZBB is not an easy process. Its effectiveness should not be exagerrated with unrealistic promises about what it can provide. Business firms should explore this useful management tool, weigh its costs and benefits, and then determine if ZBB would enhance their financial planning function and aid in cost control.

Finally, we conclude this chapter with the following recommended guidelines for the successful installation of the zero base budgeting process:

1. Learn about ZBB. Several members of the staff should become very familiar with ZBB literature and even attend a ZBB orientation seminar.
2. Carefully scrutinize what is really going on in the company, and analyze the needs of the company before implementing ZBB. One should ask: Is my company ready for ZBB? Do we have a good accounting system? Can we get full support from top management?
3. Strategic planning should always precede the zero base budgeting process. Communicate to all levels of management the goals and objectives and provide a clearer assignment of responsibility for justifying expenditures and setting priorities.
4. Define required resources before implementation. This includes obtaining adequate staff within the budgeting department, setting up a top management steering committee, appointing local budget coordinators, and fixing responsibility for the various steps for all concerned individuals and groups.
5. Develop a budget calendar, define certain policies and procedures, and design a ZBB method tailored to the company's specific environment.
6. Allow adequate time for training budget personnel and users. Encourage all levels of management participation, especially top management's cooperation and commitment.
7. Consider a pilot project approach; that is, test ZBB in a small segment of the company before implementing it throughout the organization. This approach allows mistakes to be corrected without publicity and fanfare.

3
The Decision Package

The first issue that a newcomer to zero base budgeting is confronted with is something called a *decision package.* In most instances, this term is a misnomer because the package is really a single piece of paper completed on only one side which hardly constitutes a package. However, in larger, more structured organizations, the amount of information required to make a decision on a given activity will require a considerable amount of information, hence the term *package.* A word of caution: keep the package as small and as brief as possible. The less information required and the smaller the package, the less resistance your staff will have to properly completing it because it will be less of a burden. The average manager probably needs several days to fill out the minimum required for his unit's activities and, therefore, if a piece of information would be nice to have but is not critical to the decision process, leave it off.

This chapter discusses the process of decision package preparation. The first part describes how to identify decision units within the MIS function. The second section discusses the analysis of each decision unit in terms of decision unit objectives, description of current operations, workload and performance measurements, alternatives, and incremental analysis. Next, the typical decision package format, contents, and example packages are presented. Finally, the relationship between the decision packages and the final budget is described.

IDENTIFICATION OF DECISION UNITS

Zero base budgeting attempts to focus management's attention on evaluating activities and making decisions, and, therefore, the basic ingredients of ZBB, the decision units within the organization, must be identified and defined. A decision unit is a tangible activity or group of activities that management considers for planning, analysis, and review. There is no uniform method of identifying a decision unit. The unit can be the traditional cost center or budget unit or it can encompass a group of people performing similar activities. Decision units may also include special projects or programs, service received or provided, capital expenditures, or cost recovery programs.

Cost centers or budget units are the traditional and most widely used focus of decision packages. They usually correspond with the established organization chart and are easily subdividable into smaller identifiable functions or activities. For example, a single cost center of the MIS department might be divided into systems, programming, operations, and control functions.

Decision packages may be built around people acting as a group and performing similar activities. A computer control and security staff, application programming group, or computer operations staff are examples.

Decision packages may be focused on MIS projects. For example, a project title may be "Branch Operating and Information Systems." The major objective of this project is to design a management information system that will optimize the branch operating cost structure, branch functions, and branch/head office data flow in order to improve customer and dealer service, to enhance the efficiency of the sales support systems, and to increase the branch's profit. The project may call for wages and salaries, materials or supplies, capital expenditures, and different types of support expenditures such as travel or insurance.

Decision packages may be developed with respect to the MIS service received or services provided. If the company hires an outside consultant to provide MIS service to a new project, a separate decision package may be prepared for service received. On the other hand, a company such as a bank may provide services for both itself and for its customers as a computer service bureau. In this case, separate decision packages should be prepared for services provided.

Decision packages may also be developed for MIS capital expenditures and cost recovery programs. Examples of capital expenditures include new stand-alone minicomputer or microcomputer systems or communication systems. Cost recovery programs include a review of the computer load and a plan to sell computer time and computer-supported service, a review of available computer systems such as payroll, accounts receivable, accounts payable, and a plan to market the systems and related services.

ANALYSIS OF EACH DECISION UNIT

Once the decision units have been identified, each must be analyzed for determination of the basic requirements and increments. Stonich (1977) recommended that the managers analyze each decision unit in terms of: (1) decision unit objectives, (2) description of current operation, (3) workload and performance measurements, (4) alternatives, and (5) incremental analysis.

A decision unit manager begins the analysis by specifying his objective and the purpose of the decision unit. Stating the objectives of the function in a meaningful way is probably one of the most difficult tasks of preparing decision packages. Yet a clear statement is essential to the whole process. The statement should not be a list of current activities but a statement of purpose. Generally, it should indicate what the decision unit will do with the resources provided. An example of an MIS decision unit objective might be to provide management with a timely and reliable management information system and to transform the users' needs into workable and manageable systems.

After writing the decision unit objectives, the manager describes how the unit currently operates and the resources utilized, identifying both personnel and other supporting costs. Are the resources required to support the current activities justified? What resources used are outside the decision unit manager's control? What coordination is necessary between decision units?

Workload and performance measurements are then developed to examine the relative strengths and weaknesses of the decision unit manager's current approach and to further describe his objective in great detail. Examples of performance measurement for computer systems include the accuracy of reports, turnaround time, number of projects completed, and number of programs implemented.

The decision unit manager next considers alternative methods of operating. He should identify and evaluate all meaningful alternatives and choose the one(s) he considers the best. The following questions may be used as a guide in considering alternative methods:

1. Should the activity be performed in the same way in view of current operating conditions?
2. Can the task be done in a different way at less cost?

3. Can another decision unit or an outside organization perform the task better or at less cost?
4. Can any activities profitably be combined with others?

If an alternative to the current method of doing business is chosen, the recommended method should be shown in the decision package with the current method shown as the alternative *not recommended.*

Incremental analysis can begin after the best alternative has been selected. Incremental packages reflect different levels of effort for performing the operation. One package, the "base package," may establish a minimum level of activity and others may identify higher levels of activity or cost. The minimum level of effort must be below the current level of effort. The manager should identify the minimum, critical level of effort below which the activity should be discontinued because it loses viability. The following questions may be used as a guide in performing incremental analysis:

1. For the best alternative, what is the minimum, critical level of effort (the first increment) that must be performed to provide only the "bare bones" essential services and outputs?
2. What additional, incremental efforts would have to be added to the minimum level of effort to come up to the current level? This could be a single increment or two or three increments.
3. If expansion beyond the current level is advisable, what additional increment is cost justified?

An example of a data processing department analysis is presented in Figure 3.1

PREPARATION OF DECISION PACKAGES

After the manager has analyzed each decision unit, he must prepare decision packages. The decision package is the building block of the zero base budgeting concept. It is a document that identifies and describes each activity in such a manner that managers can evaluate it, rank it against other activities, and decide whether to approve or disapprove its funding.

There is no such thing as a "standard" decision package format. Decision package formats will vary widely among organizations and

Objective: To develop, implement, and maintain computer systems designed to meet the needs of the corporation. To schedule and run computer reports in a timely fashion.

Current operations and required resources: There are six employees involved in data processing. Two are involved in systems development design and testing, and three are maintaining existing systems. One is the manager of the department. The systems development workload will increase substantially for 6 to 10 months and then decrease. With the completion of the development project, there will be a commensurate increase in operations work. The current total for salaries is $100,800 a year.

Support: The data processing department relies on the entire accounting group for source information. Systems design information is primarily provided by the controller and line management personnel.

Workload measurement:

1. Delays in implementing new systems.
2. Delays in printing output from existing systems.

Performance measurement:

1. Variance from scheduled completion dates – 2 weeks.
2. Turnaround time for output from production systems – 3 days.
3. Accuracy of reports – 95%.

Alternatives:

1. Contract with a service bureau rather than retain an in-house data processing capability.
2. Design capability for online, real-time information system.
3. Seek ways to further computerize existing systems for faster information availability.

Increments:

Number	Description	Expense	Employees
1 of 4	Employ programmer, analyst, computer operator, data clerk, and manager (minimum level)	$142,000	5
2 of 4	Add data control clerk (current level)	12,000	6
3 of 4	Add one programmer	24,000	7
4 of 4	Add computer operator	15,000	8

Figure 3.1. Data processing department analysis.

you must therefore design one that fits your own needs. The contents of the decision packages usually includes:

1. Objective, purpose, and scope
2. What is to be done and how
3. Consequences of not doing the activity

4. Alternative methods
5. Alternative levels of effort
6. Costs and benefits of recommended alternative methods and levels
7. Resources required

Figure 3.2 is an example of a decision package that was used by Management Information Services and Figure 3.3 presents an example of a completed decision package for a new computer billing system. These packages were developed during the company's 1979 zero base budgeting process. The following list describes each part of this decision package example.

1. Department: The name of the organizational unit responsible for performing the indicated activity. Typically the department is headed up by a management-level person who is responsible for directing and setting the priorities of the activities of the staff. The department is identical to the decision unit described above. Examples include programming manager, keypunch supervisor, and data center manager.
2. Activity No.: A means of identifying this activity that, together with the activity level (below), uniquely identifies the decision package.
3. Activity Level: Used in conjunction with the activity number (above). On many occasions it is necessary or desirable to break apart the activity into several subsets. In the example shown in Figure 3.3, the computer billing system activity actually had five levels which included development of a new system as well as maintenance of the existing system. Sometimes these activities are dependent on one another, and other times they are mutually exclusive. The separation of these dependencies is covered elsewhere on the form. Alternatively, these two fields, activity number and activity level, could be combined into a field entitled "package number 134–5."
4. Project/continuing Activity: Distinguishes one-time activities from the on-going ones. For example, keypunching payroll time cards is a continuing activity, whereas rewriting the

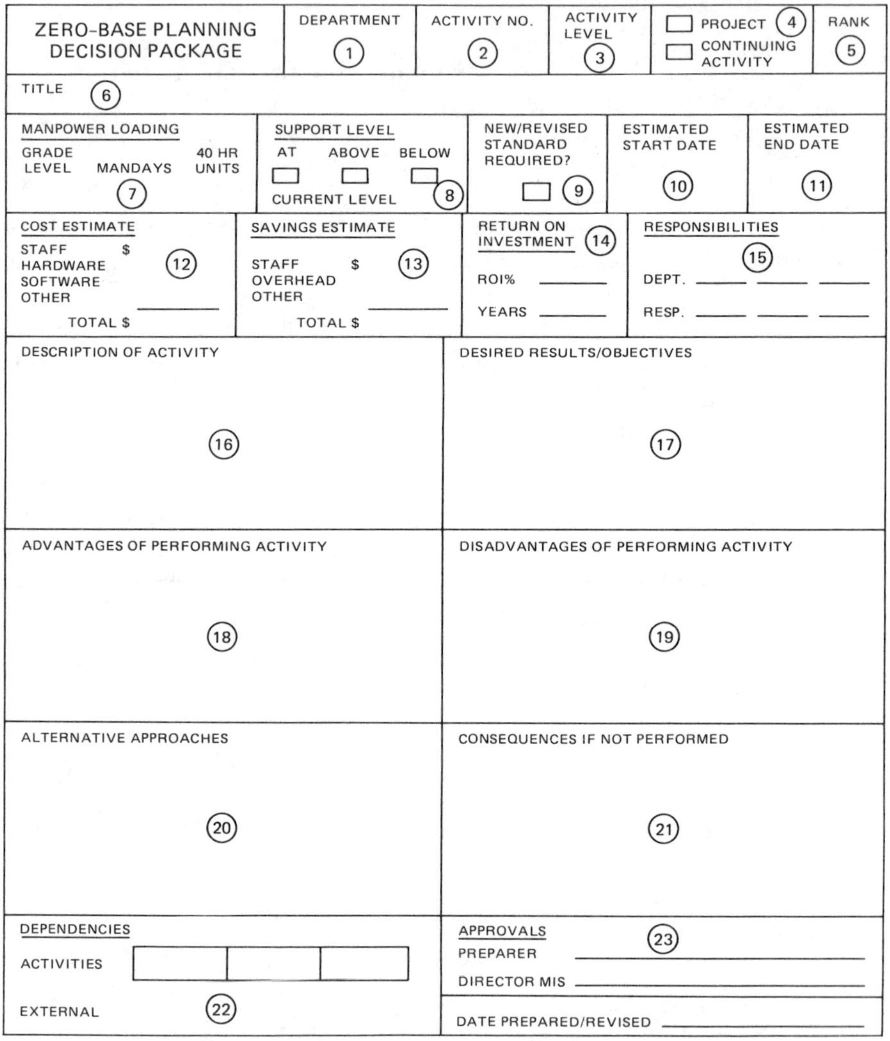

Figure 3.2. Sample decision package (Management Information Services).

payroll system would be considered a project despite the fact that the rewrite project never seems to come to an end.

5. Rank: A number from one to six that specifies the priority assigned to the decision package (see Figure 4.1).
6. Title: A brief name for the activity being described by the package. Brevity is again recommended because the title may be used in computerized reporting (see Chapter 7).

ZERO-BASE PLANNING DECISION PACKAGE	DEPARTMENT Programming 01	ACTIVITY NO. 134	ACTIVITY LEVEL 5	[X] PROJECT [ ] CONTINUING ACTIVITY	RANK 6

TITLE Computer Billing System

MANPOWER LOADING			SUPPORT LEVEL	NEW/REVISED STANDARD REQUIRED?	ESTIMATED START DATE	ESTIMATED END DATE
GRADE LEVEL	MANDAYS	40 HR UNITS	AT [ ] ABOVE [X] BELOW [ ]			
34	230	1	CURRENT LEVEL	[X]	5-1-79	2-1-80
35	230	1				

COST ESTIMATE		SAVINGS ESTIMATE		RETURN ON INVESTMENT		RESPONSIBILITIES
STAFF	$ 88,575	STAFF	$ 5,000	ROI%	6	DEPT.
HARDWARE		OVERHEAD		YEARS	18	RESP.
SOFTWARE		OTHER				
OTHER						
TOTAL $	88,575	TOTAL $	5,000			

DESCRIPTION OF ACTIVITY

Design and install a new billing system that utilizes software physics theory, product pricing, and natural business unit pricing.

DESIRED RESULTS/OBJECTIVES

Be cost effective.
Change to fit evolving technology.
Provide for incentive pricing.

ADVANTAGES OF PERFORMING ACTIVITY

Attain competitive pricing position.
Incentive pricing will encourage users to adopt less expensive technologies.

DISADVANTAGES OF PERFORMING ACTIVITY

Will require a product costing system.

ALTERNATIVE APPROACHES

Bill each computer run utilizing a single usage rate.

CONSEQUENCES IF NOT PERFORMED

Continued dependency upon occupancy time billing.

DEPENDENCIES

ACTIVITIES 134-4

EXTERNAL Adoption of new pricing policies

APPROVALS

PREPARER ______

DIRECTOR MIS ______

DATE PREPARED/REVISED 7/1/79

Figure 3.3. Computer billing system decision package.

7. Manpower Loading: Identifies the level of effort required by various types of individuals. In the example shown in Figure 3.3, a senior programmer and a senior systems analyst, grades 34 and 35, respectively, will be required for one man-year each. This section can get quite complicated depending upon how the jobs are structured and what happens when higher-

powered or less-experienced individuals are actually assigned to the project or continuing activity. The result can be a different total cost. In many chargeout systems, a single rate per hour is used regardless of the level of staff assigned to it. In more complex systems, the chargeout rate is based on the level of the individual doing the work. Refer to Chapter 8 for a further discussion of chargeout systems.

8. Support Level: Describes whether the activity recommended is at exactly the same level of effort currently being expended, is above it, or below it. For example, the task of maintaining our standard payroll programs might require one full-time person to apply tax changes, program logic updates, and create special reports for the end user. If the recommendation is to maintain a full-time support person, one would check the "At" box. However, the manager may wish to additionally recommend that the payroll system be replaced by a purchased package in which case the maintenance level could be reduced to 50% of a person and the "Below" box would then be checked. However, given the quality of most of the payroll packages on the market today, this assumption may be shortsighted.
9. Standard Required: A reminder to the standards department that, if the activity is approved and actually begun, an operating standard may be affected or a new one may need to be written.
10. Estimated Start Date: The planned beginning of the project, which, in the case of a continuing activity is usually the start of the fiscal year.
11. Estimated End Date: The targeted completion date of the project or the last day of the fiscal year for continuing activities.
12. Cost Estimate: Shows the estimated costs of staff wages and salaries, hardware, software, and other costs such as the computer time charged to the project, outside services required, and so forth.
13. Savings Estimate: The displacement of costs affected by this activity. In our example of the computerized billing system, a decision maker could balance total costs of implementing the system against what he can save in billing clerks or service bureau costs.

14. Return on Investment (ROI): This item shows the performance measure in terms of a return on investment percentage. Alternatives to the ROI include payback years, return on assets, and the internal rate of return.
15. Responsibilities: Identifies all departments affected by, involved in, or working on this activity. In the case of our computer billing system in Figure 3.3, the programming and finance departments both participated in the development of the new billing system. The finance department was the requestor and is the end user of the system. Other types of involvement could include the role of a consultant or an approval authority. This responsibility chart is particularily good in larger data processing organizations that tend to loose sight of all the players.
16. Description of Activity: A concise narrative describing the activity/activity level that the package is prepared for. Brevity is recommended.
17. Desired Results (Objectives): The objectives should refer to some overall goals of the department rather than be just a rehash of the description. The three objectives shown in Figure 3.3 were from a list of eight general objectives for the company.
18. Advantages of Performing Activity: A few statements regarding the benefits to be obtained from performing the activity.
19. Disadvantages of Performing Activity: What are the risks or shortcomings involved?
20. Alternative Approaches: Describes what alternatives to the activity are available to the company.
21. Consequences if Activity Is Not Performed: What will happen if we do not begin the activity? Are there any legal ramifications? Is the company's market share going to suffer?
22. Dependencies: Describes certain policies that will be required from top management in order for the activity to be successful. In our computer billing system example, the new system's use of a totally different scheme of charging for computer use required top management approval before the system could be implemented. Also contained under this item is a cross-reference to other activities.

23. Approvals – Preparer: The manager responsible for the execution of this activity should sign here.
    Approvals – Director MIS: This indicates that the preparer's manager agrees with the contents of the package.

A decision package used by Continental Airlines in 1981 is shown in Figure 3.4. Without being redundant, the following informational items vary from those contained in the previous example.

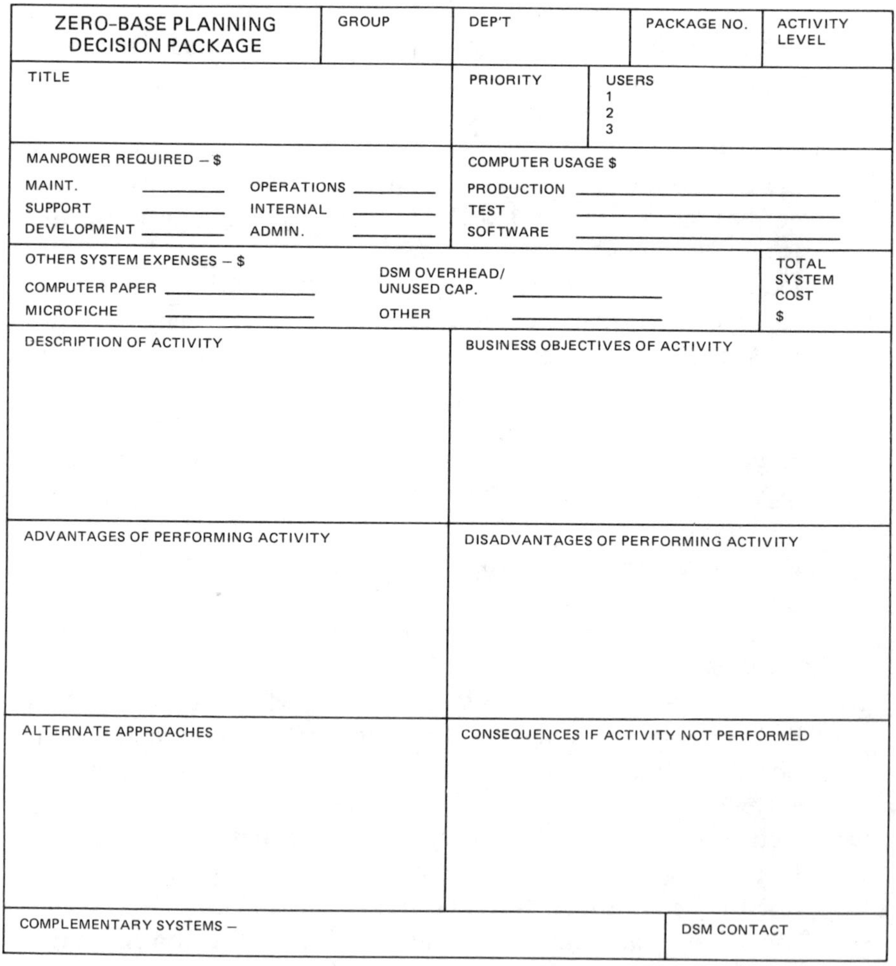

ZERO-BASE PLANNING DECISION PACKAGE | GROUP | DEP'T | PACKAGE NO. | ACTIVITY LEVEL

TITLE | PRIORITY | USERS 1 2 3

MANPOWER REQUIRED – $
MAINT. ______ OPERATIONS ______
SUPPORT ______ INTERNAL ______
DEVELOPMENT ______ ADMIN. ______

COMPUTER USAGE $
PRODUCTION ______
TEST ______
SOFTWARE ______

OTHER SYSTEM EXPENSES – $
COMPUTER PAPER ______
MICROFICHE ______
DSM OVERHEAD/ UNUSED CAP. ______
OTHER ______
TOTAL SYSTEM COST $

DESCRIPTION OF ACTIVITY | BUSINESS OBJECTIVES OF ACTIVITY

ADVANTAGES OF PERFORMING ACTIVITY | DISADVANTAGES OF PERFORMING ACTIVITY

ALTERNATE APPROACHES | CONSEQUENCES IF ACTIVITY NOT PERFORMED

COMPLEMENTARY SYSTEMS – | DSM CONTACT

Figure 3.4. Sample decision package (Continental Airlines).

Group: A subset of the department level. Examples include the financial systems group and the reservations system group and correspond to the decision unit described earlier.

Package Number: Identical to the activity number

Priority: Identical to rank

Users: Similar to responsibility. Sometimes referred to as *sponsor.*

Manpower Required/Computer Usage/Other System Expenses: These items break down the cost of the project into a finer detail than shown in Figure 3.2.

Complementary Systems: Similar to dependencies

DSM Contact: Similar to department manager

The third decision package format is shown in Figure 3.5 and is adapted from Dillon (1979, pp. 160–162). The following are instructions to fill out the information items shown in Figure 3.5:

1. Enter date submitted by the initiating supervisor or manager.
2. If the decision package consists of (or relates to) an objective included in an organization plan, enter the objective identification number.
3. Enter the short title of the activity or organization objective.
4. Indicate the level of effort here. For example, if the decision package represents the "minimum" increment of a three-level activity, enter "Level 1 of 3."
5. Self-explanatory.
6. Self-explanatory.
7. Enter the signature (or initials) of the initiating supervisor/manager and of others in the approval chain. Generally, each decision package should be approved (with respect to correctness of information) by a department-level executive.
8. Enter priority ranking assigned to the decision package. Entry should be made in pencil to permit reranking at higher consolidated levels. Assign rank no. 6 to the highest priority package.
9. Describe the activity in terms of its purpose or intended result.

DECISION PACKAGE

OBJECTIVE NO (2) DATE (1)

ACTIVITY (OR OBJECTIVE) NAME (3) LEVEL NO (4) OF	DEPARTMENT (5) DIVISION (6)	PREPARED APPROVED (7)	RANK (8)

PURPOSE OF ACTIVITY (9) / DESCRIPTION OF ACTIVITY (10)	RESOURCES REQUIRED		CURRENT YEAR	BUDGET YEAR
PURPOSE OF ACTIVITY (9)	PERSONNEL			(14)
	LABOR	($)		(15)
DESCRIPTION OF ACTIVITY (10)	OUTSIDE SERVICES	($)		(16)
	OTHER	($)		(17)
	TOTAL	($)		(18)

ALTERNATIVE WAYS OF PERFORMING WORK OR PROGRAM AND COSTS (11)

ADVANTAGES OF RETAINING ACTIVITY (12)

CONSEQUENCES IF ACTIVITY IS ELIMINATED (13)

Figure 3.5. Sample decision package. Reprinted from *Zero-base Budgeting for Health Care Institutions* by R.D. Dillion by permission of Aspen Systems Corporation, © 1979.

10. Describe the activity in terms of the means or process by which the activity is to be accomplished.
11. Where different ways of performing the activity have been evaluated, briefly describe the alternatives and the reasons why they were rejected. For example, if the decision package provides for the performance of a service in-house, why was the outside purchase rejected?
12. State the principal benefits that will accrue to the organization if the activity is retained (funded). Describe benefits to your own organization *and* other organizations that are affected.
13. State the consequences that will result if the activity is eliminated (not funded). Distinguish between the consequences to your own and to another organization.

14–18. Fill in all applicable figures for the budget year. If current-year (expected) information is not readily available, provide a reasonable estimate. To avoid misinterpretation, identify all data representing a partial year by indicating the number of months in parentheses. Round dollar figures to the nearest $100.

14. Enter the number of employees (or full-time equivalent employees) required to perform the activity.
15. Enter the payroll costs of the activity.
16. Enter the cost of major outside services, if any. Minor outside services should be included in no. 17.
17. Enter the amount of other costs here.
18. Total should equal the sum of items 15, 16, and 17.

The appendix at the end of this chapter presents 3 more types of decision packages and 10 completed decision packages relating specifically to MIS activities.

Once the format and contents of the decision package are decided upon, the next task is to decide who will be directly involved in the completion of the packages for each activity. The process will be a lengthy one requiring a good deal of insight and creativity. One of the obvious people that should be involved is the first-line manager responsible for the execution of the activity. This individual might carry the title "programming manager" or "keypunch supervisor" and has the lowest level of management authority. Senior staff members and project leaders could assist in the initial completion task. Other departments involved in the activity, especially the end user, should have an opportunity to contribute to the content of the packages and could even be given approval authority. At this phase of the project, the rank or priority number should not be addressed. The creativity of the individual completing the form comes into play when one must identify alternatives to known activities as well as new activities not currently identified. For example, an activity that would obtain a TSO terminal for each programmer might be something in the uppermost mind of the programming manager but is considered to be out of the question by the hardware manager because of resource limitations. If there is even a remote possibility of justification this year or next, a package should be completed.

If the Management Information Services Department has a current strategic plan, be sure to address all of the issues included: weaknesses, strengths, threats, and opportunities. If you have a long-range project plan, include all of those projects in decision packages. Additional types of activities could include research and development projects and requirements definition projects as well as expanded administrative functions. For example, with the advent of intelligent copiers and office-of-the-future technology, whoever is responsible for the acquisition and support of office functions and office copiers should report to data processing. It is not too farfetched to extend this approach to the mail room, given the recent advances and directions of electronic mail systems.

An alternative to this approach is the redefinition of the MIS function into three areas: (1) data processing, (2) data management, and (3) office support.

BALANCE AGAINST EXISTING BUDGET

After the decision packages are prepared, it is necessary to balance those identified activities that are currently taking place against the department's current budget. This is the only way to ensure that the activity costs and manpower estimates have any resemblance to the real world. Questions of credibility will be raised without this step.

In order to accomplish this task, separate the activity packages into various cost centers or departments and put aside those packages marked "Above" current levels. The computer can make this task easier. (See Chapter 7 for further discussion.) Add up the total manpower and total dollars and balance against the individual cost center budget. To increase the accuracy, the decision packages should be further subdivided by level of individual required or other major cost items. The result of this process is then summarized in a schedule prepared for each department as, for instance, in Figure 3.6. In this example, four decision packages were prepared for decision unit XYZ that are "Below" or "At" current levels of effort. The sum of each column in Figure 3.6 represents the total costs for each decision package, and the sum of each row represents the budget line item of each major expenditure.

If any large discrepancies exist, one should review the individual activities, costs, and manpower estimates. Perhaps a given activity

Expenditure \ Activity	No. 1	No. 2	No. 3	No. 4	Total
Salaries	$20,000	$10,000	$ 8,000	$	$38,000
Employee Taxes	4,000	2,000	1,500	–	7,500
Supplies	1,000	500	400	–	1,900
Travel	1,000	–	–	–	1,000
Insurance	500	--	–	–	500
Miscellaneous	3,500	2,500	100	5,000	11,100
Total	$30,000	$15,000	$10,000	$5,000	$60,000

Figure 3.6. Reconciliation to current budget, decision unit: XYZ.

requires more effort than originally thought. The activity cost must also include a burden rate for the MIS overhead. Each department should be balanced in this manner and then all departments combined and balanced to the MIS plan. Unless you have a very large shop with complicated computer usage chargeout procedures, it would not be worth your effort to include computer usage costs in your programming rate. The cost of testing can be classified as overhead and applied to the general computer rates. Be careful not to double count these expenses. Once the current activities are balanced against the department's budget and the manpower and cost indicated for each activity are deemed reasonable, it is then proper to review the remainder of the activities and make adjustments to the estimated costs similar to the corrections made above.

Appendix

Sample Forms and Decision Packages

Several different decision package formats were depicted in Chapter 3. This appendix presents additional forms and completed examples of MIS decision packages.

Companies and Forms	*Exhibits*
General Radio	1 and 2
Bekins Company	3
Southern California Edison Co.	4 and 5
BCS Richland, Inc. – Minicomputer Example	6
Xerox Corporation – Data Capsule	7 and 8
St. Anne-Nackawic Pulp and Paper Company, Ltd. Data Processing Department	9
Management Information Serv. – Install VM	10
Management Information Serv. – Maintain General Ledger	11
Management Information Serv. – Maintain Systems Control Program	12
X Company – Systems Production Control	13
Y Company – VSAM Support	14
Y Company – Data Manager Support	15
Y Company – Data Communications Support	16

General Radio

DECISION PACKAGE COVER SHEET
ZERO-BASE BUDGETING OVERHEAD

1

(8) RANK

INCREMENT ___ OF ___

$(000)

(1) DECISION UNIT NAME

(2) CORPORATE UNIT

(3) LEVEL A ORGANIZATION UNIT

(4) LEVEL B ORGANIZATION UNIT(S)

(5) LEVEL C ORGANIZATION UNIT(S)

(6) PREPARED BY

(7) DATE

(9) DESCRIBE CURRENT SERVICES PROVIDED, RESOURCES USED, DIRECT CLIENTS OF SERVICE, AND HOW THE DECISION UNIT OPERATES.

(10) DESCRIBE DESIRED MEANS OF ACCOMPLISHING THIS DECISION UNIT'S GOALS

(11) LIST DISCARDED ALTERNATIVE MEANS OF ACCOMPLISHING THIS DECISION UNIT'S GOALS AND REASONS FOR DISCARDING ALTERNATIVES

(12) SUMMARY OF DECISION PACKAGE INCREMENTS	1976 PROJECTED						
	POSITIONS		OPERATING EXPENSES			CAPITAL EXPENSES CUM 1976	INVENT COM CUM 1976
	1976 INCR	1976 CUM	1976 INCR	1976 CUM	% CUM 76, 78		
1 of							
2 of							
3 of							
4 of							
5 of							
6 of							

Exhibit 3.1. Adapted from Hill 1977, p. 15.

General Radio INCREMENT ____ OF ____

ZERO-BASE BUDGETING OVERHEAD

MINIMUM LEVEL OF EFFORT INCREMENTAL ANALYSIS $(000)

(1) DECISION UNIT NAME

(14) DESCRIBE OPERATIONS PERFORMED AND SERVICES PROVIDED

(13) RESOURCES REQUIRED	1974 ACI	1975 BUDG	1975 PROJ	1976 PROP
POSITIONS THIS INCREMENT				
POSITIONS CUMULATIVE				
OPERATING EXPENSE THIS INCREMENT				
OPERATING EXPENSE CUMULATIVE				
OPERATING EXPENSE % PRIOR YEAR				
CAPTIAL EXPENSE THIS INCREMENT				
CAPITAL EXPENSE CUMULATIVE				
INVENTORY COMMITMENT THIS INCREMENT				
INVENTORY COMMITMENT CUMULATIVE				

(15) DESCRIBE CHANGES FROM CURRENT OPERATIONS

(16) DESCRIBE BENEFITS OF APPROVING THIS INCREMENT

(17) OPERATING EXPENSES % 76/75 FOR MINIMUM LEVEL OF EFFORT
REASONS WHY LOWER LEVEL OF EFFORT WAS NOT CHOSEN

(18) WORKLOAD/PERFORMANCE MEASUREMENTS	1974 ACI	1975 PROJ	1976 THIS INCR	1976 CUM	% CUM. OF 1975

Exhibit 3.2. Adapted from Hill 1977, p. 16.

ZBB DECISION PACKAGE

<table>
<tr><td colspan="2">DEPARTMENT</td><td>ACTIVITY NO.</td><td>SUB NO.</td><td colspan="2">RANK</td></tr>
<tr><td colspan="2">TITLE</td><td colspan="2">☐ PROJECT
☐ ONGOING</td><td colspan="2">COST ☐ PER MO.
$</td></tr>
<tr><td colspan="2">RESOURCE RATE X MAN DAYS = COST
1.
2.
3.
4.</td><td>SUPPORT:
☐ AT
☐ ABOVE
☐ BELOW
CURRENT LEVEL</td><td colspan="3">DEPENDENCIES/ACTIVITY NOS.</td></tr>
<tr><td colspan="2">ACTIVITY DESCRIPTION</td><td colspan="4">DESIRED RESULTS (OBJECTIVES)</td></tr>
<tr><td colspan="2">ADVANTAGES OF PERFORMING ACTIVITY</td><td colspan="4">DISADVANTAGES OF PERFORMING ACTIVITY</td></tr>
<tr><td colspan="2">ALTERNATIVE APPROACHES</td><td colspan="4">CONSEQUENCES IF NOT PERFORMED</td></tr>
<tr><td>PREPARED BY</td><td>DATE</td><td colspan="3">APPROVED BY</td><td>DATE</td></tr>
</table>

Exhibit 3.3. ZBB decision package (The Bekins Company).

Southern California Edison Company (Rosemead, Calif.)

DECISION PACKAGE FORM (Front)

OBJECTIVE NO ______________ DATE ______________________

ACTIVITY (OR OBJECTIVE) NAME LEVEL NO OF	DEPARTMENT DIVISION	PREPARED APPROVED	RANK

PURPOSE OF ACTIVITY	RESOURCES REQUIRED	CURRENT YEAR	BUDGET YEAR
	PERSONNEL		
	LABOR ($)		
DESCRIPTION OF ACTIVITY	OUTSIDE SERVICES ($)		
	OTHER ($)		
	TOTAL ($)		

ALTERNATIVE WAYS OF PERFORMING WORK OR PROGRAM AND COSTS

ADVANTAGES OF RETAINING ACTIVITY

CONSEQUENCES IF ACTIVITY IS ELIMINATED

Exhibit 3.4 Southern California Edison Company decision package form (front). Reprinted, by permission of the publisher, from Zero-Base Budgeting Comes of Age by Logan M. Cheek, p. 234, © 1977 by AMACOM, a division of American Management Associations, New York. All rights reserved.

Southern California Edison Company (*Rosemead, Calif.*)

DECISION PACKAGE FORM (Back)

BUDGET YEAR EXPENDITURE DETAIL ($)			
FUNCTION NO.	LABOR	OTHER	TOTAL
Plant Work Orders			
TOTAL			

BUDGET YEAR COST DISTRIBUTION ($)		
FUNCTIONS	Operation and Maintenance – Including O/H	
	Research and Development – Expense	
	Other – Including O/H to Const. & Misc.	
	TOTAL	
PLANT WORK ORDERS	Reserach and Development – Capitalized	
	Other	
	TOTAL	
GRAND TOTAL EXPENDITURES		

Exhibit 3.5. Southern California Edison Company decision package form (back). Reprinted, by permission of the publisher, from Zero-Base Budgeting Comes of Age by Logan M. Cheek, p. 235, © 1977 by AMACOM, a division of American Management Associations, New York. All rights reserved.

BCS Richland, Inc. DECISION PACKAGE

DECISION PACKAGE IDENTIFICATION	SUPPLEMENTAL IDENTIFICATION
LEVEL 1 Data Center	DEPT. TITLE Data Center
LEVEL 2 WHC	ORGN. NO. 125200
LEVEL 3 Minicomputer Operation	RANKING NO. 116
LEVEL 4 Operators & Keypunch	
LEVEL OF SERVICE 1 of 2	

SENS CODE	LIQ	NON-LIQ	INTERDEPT	SPEC BILL
	X			

DEPT. CODE:	WBS CODE: LVL 1	LVL 2	LVL 3	LVL 4		LVL SVC	TYPE	SENS CODE
1 2 5 2 0 0	0 2	0 4	2 4	1 6		1	L	

DECISION PACKAGE TITLE (30 DIGIT MAX.)
400 Area Minicomputer 1 OF 2

DECISION PACKAGE DESCRIPTION
Operate the Data General Eclipse E300 located in the 400 (FFTF) area. This IWA describes a two-shift operation with one lead operator in charge of data control, 2 computer operators (1 days, 1 on swing) and 2 keypunch operators.

RESOURCE REQUIREMENT	FY 77	FY 78	FY 79
FULL-TIME WORKYEARS	5	5	5
LABOR DOLLARS		76,992	92,285
NON-LABOR DOLLARS			
TOTAL		76,992	92,285
CAPITAL EQUIPMENT			

JUSTIFICATION
The minicomputer is operated by BCSR under contract to WHC in support of the Bechtel FFTF construction activity. Present major programs are Bechtel Payroll and Engineering Indices.

CONSEQUENCES OF NOT PERFORMING
Bechtel or WHC would have to take over the mini operation.

ALTERNATIVES
Bechtel could manage this operation as they did prior to 6/77 when it was handled by terminal access to a remote computer. WHC requested BCSR to take over the operation when the change was made to a minicomputer. BCSR has the capability of providing backup operators for vacation or illness, thereby providing a more cost-effective organization.

PREPARED BY ____________ DATE ____________

DEPARTMENT MANAGER APPROVAL [signature] DATE 1/19/77

REVISION DATE ____________

Exhibit 3.6. Minicomputer. Reprinted, by permission of the publisher, from Zero-Base Budgeting Comes of Age by Logan M. Cheek, p. 57 © 1977 by AMACOM, a division of American Management Associations, New York. All rights reserved.

Xerox Corporation (Rochester, N.Y.)

DECISION PACKAGE (page 1)

(1) PROGRAM NAME	(2) DEPARTMENT	(3) BUDGET CENTER	(4) YEAR	(5) RANKING
Data Capsule	ISG Region Operations Mgt.	F698	73/74	

(6) STATEMENT OF PURPOSE

Provide accurate run length Data Base of installed equipment

(7) DESCRIPTION OF ACTIONS (OPERATIONS)

Salesman completes label—installs Data Capsule
Mail in preaddressed envelope to Rochester
Rochester logs—enters header
Translator—Data Base
Report mailed back to salesman—data stored for reference

(8) PROGRAM BENEFITS

Customer Satisfaction
Sales Effectiveness
Professionalism—No guessing on the best Price Plan
Reduced Cancellations—Right copier for a given volume
Additional Business—Documentation for trade-up or accessory
Data Base for ISG (Pricing, etc.)

(9) MANPOWER REQUIRED

	TBA
3 Exempts	MacKenzie
2 Non-Exempts	Hagedorn
	Irving
	Kunes
	Fitzhugh

(10) RESOURCE SUMMARY ($ IN THE THOUSANDS)	1973	1974	1975
TOTAL EXPENSES	$242	$194	
MANPOWER: EXEMPT	3	3	
NON-EXEMPT	2	2	

Exhibit 3.7. Data capsule. Reprinted, by permission of the publisher, from Zero-Base Budgeting Comes of Age by Logan M. Cheek, p. 248, ©1977 by AMACOM, a division of American Management Associations, New York. All right reserved.

Xerox Corporation (Rochester, N.Y.)

DECISION PACKAGE (page 2)

(1) PROGRAM NAME	(2) DEPARTMENT	(3) BUDGET CENTER	(4) YEAR	(5) RANKING
Data Capsule	ISG Region Operations Mgt.	S698	73/74	

(11) COST ASSUMPTION WORKSHEET OF NON-LABOR COSTS

General Travel

16 trips (8 trips MacKenzie, 8 trips Hagedorn)
$2250 per trip

XDX Equipment Maintenance

1973 Go Out-Transfer agreement
$1605 X 12 months = $19260

Dues and Subscriptions

1974-400 Data Capsule Units @ $120 = $48,000
1973-800 Data Capsule Units @ $120 = $96,000

(12) OTHER UNIQUE COSTS

Depreciation

4 year straight line on Sigma 3 mainframe
$107,000/4 years = $26,750

(13) DETAILED COSTING ($ THOUSANDS)

	Account	1973	1974
	Wages & Salaries	$95	$95
	Travel	4	4
	XDX Equip Maint	20	20
	Dues & Subs.	96	48
	XDX Depreciation	27	27
	Total	$242	$194

(14) 1974 CALENDARIZATION

QUARTER	1	2	3	4
EXPENSES	$86	$36	$36	$36
MANPOWER: EXEMPT	3	3	3	3
NON-EXEMPT	2	2	2	2

Exhibit 3.8. Data capsule, cont'd. Reprinted, by permission of the publisher, from Zero-Base Budgeting Comes of Age by Logan M. Cheek, p. 249, © 1977 by AMACOM, a division of American Management Associations, New York. All rights reserved.

St. Anne-Nackawic Pulp & Paper Company, Ltd. DECISION PACKAGE, LEVEL 2

DECISION PACKAGE | CODE: C22 | RANK: 31

OBJECTIVE OR ACTIVITY:
Data Processing LEVEL 2 OF 2

DEPARTMENT: Finance

RANKING OF OTHER LEVELS: 14

DESIRED RESULTS:
To provide an acceptable level of program maintenance.
To provide an adequate level of supervision of union staff.
Some new systems development would be done. Produce reports when required.

DESCRIPTION OF ACTIVITY:
Use part-time keypuncher to handle peak loads.
Make changes to existing programs and systems on a timely basis.
Analysis and programming of new systems as time allows.

RESOURCES REQUIRED	CURRENT YEAR	BUDGET YEAR THIS LEVEL	BUDGET YEAR ACCUM.	% OF CURRENT YEAR
PERSONNEL (NON-UNION/UNION) #	2/3	1/0	2/3	
(NON-UNION) $	59,000	25,000	66,300	112
(UNION) $	56,600	4,000	60,200	106
OUTSIDE $	20,000	–	–	0
SUPPLIES $	9,900	3,000	12,000	121
RENTALS $	54,500	–	55,500	102
TOTAL $	200,000	32,000	194,000	97

HOW AND WHEN ACCOMPLISHED:
Utilize part-time keypuncher to handle peak loads at critical times (month, quarter, and year end) and for special jobs.
Programmer-Analyst to make changes to existing programs and systems to reflect changing company policy or requirements and to satisfy legal requirements.
On a priority basis and as time allows, do systems analysis and write programs to relieve present manual systems and provide statistics which are not now available.

OTHER OPTIONS/ALTERNATIVES TO ACHIEVE SAME OR PARTIAL RESULTS:
Schedule overtime for Keypunch Operators.
Contract new development work to outside consultants.

ADVANTAGES OF RETAINING ACTIVITY:
Use of part-time Keypuncher allows reports to be produced in the current time frames.
Some time will be available to do anlaysis and programming for those areas not now computereized (as operations).
Backup will be provided for the superintendent's position.
Present systems would be kept in a current and useful state.

CONSEQUENCES IF ACTIVITY IS ELIMINATED:
New systems would have to be contracted to an outside source and the cost would be greater than this level.
The present systems would deteriorate to a level where they are no longer reliable or useful.
Reports such as costs, General Ledgers, and A.R. would not be issued in the current time frames.

PREPARED BY: B.L. DATE: April 7/77 | APPROVED BY: DATE:

Exhibit 3.9. Data processing department. Reprinted, by permission of the publisher, from Zero-Base Budgeting Comes of Age by Logan M. Cheek, p. 128,

ZERO-BASE PLANNING DECISION PACKAGE	DEPARTMENT Tech Services 02	ACTIVITY NO. 201	ACTIVITY LEVEL 2	[X] PROJECT [ ] CONTINUING ACTIVITY	RANK 3

TITLE Install VM

MANPOWER LOADING	SUPPORT LEVEL	NEW/REVISED STANDARD REQUIRED?	ESTIMATED START DATE	ESTIMATED END DATE
GRADE LEVEL 35, MANDAYS 400, 40 HR UNITS 2	AT [ ] ABOVE [X] BELOW [ ] CURRENT LEVEL	[ ]	7-1-78	12-31-78

COST ESTIMATE	SAVINGS ESTIMATE	RETURN ON INVESTMENT	RESPONSIBILITIES
STAFF $ HARDWARE SOFTWARE OTHER ______ TOTAL $	STAFF $ OVERHEAD OTHER ______ TOTAL $	ROI% ______ YEARS ______	DEPT. ______ ______ ______ RESP. ______ ______ ______

DESCRIPTION OF ACTIVITY	DESIRED RESULTS/OBJECTIVES
Convert operating system to VM	Upgrade operating system to remain state of the art

ADVANTAGES OF PERFORMING ACTIVITY	DISADVANTAGES OF PERFORMING ACTIVITY
Remain state of the art. Increased vendor support.	No short term payback

ALTERNATIVE APPROACHES	CONSEQUENCES IF NOT PERFORMED
Remain on MVS	Potential future loss of MVS support

DEPENDENCIES	APPROVALS
ACTIVITIES 201-1	PREPARER ______ DIRECTOR MIS ______
EXTERNAL None	DATE PREPARED/REVISED 7/1/78

Exhibit 3.10. Install VM (Management Information Services).

ZERO-BASE PLANNING DECISION PACKAGE	DEPARTMENT Programming 01	ACTIVITY NO. 141	ACTIVITY LEVEL 1	☐ PROJECT ☒ CONTINUING ACTIVITY	RANK 5

TITLE Maintain General Ledger

MANPOWER LOADING			SUPPORT LEVEL			NEW/REVISED STANDARD REQUIRED?	ESTIMATED START DATE	ESTIMATED END DATE
GRADE LEVEL	MANDAYS	40 HR UNITS	AT	ABOVE	BELOW			
35	100	.5	☒	☐	☐	☐	1-1-78	12-31-78
			CURRENT LEVEL					

COST ESTIMATE		SAVINGS ESTIMATE		RETURN ON INVESTMENT		RESPONSIBILITIES	
STAFF	$	STAFF	$	ROI%		DEPT.	
HARDWARE		OVERHEAD		YEARS		RESP.	
SOFTWARE		OTHER	10,000				
OTHER		TOTAL $	10,000				
TOTAL $							

DESCRIPTION OF ACTIVITY	DESIRED RESULTS/OBJECTIVES
Maintain vendor general ledger package.	Keep package software current.

ADVANTAGES OF PERFORMING ACTIVITY	DISADVANTAGES OF PERFORMING ACTIVITY
Will stay current with vendor ensuring better support.	None

ALTERNATIVE APPROACHES	CONSEQUENCES IF NOT PERFORMED
Do not implement enhancements	Live with existing system capabilities. Eliminate system.

DEPENDENCIES	APPROVALS
ACTIVITIES	PREPARER
	DIRECTOR MIS
EXTERNAL None	DATE PREPARED/REVISED 7/1/78

Exhibit 3.11. Maintain general ledger (Management Information Services).

ZERO-BASE PLANNING DECISION PACKAGE	DEPARTMENT Tech Services 02	ACTIVITY NO. 201	ACTIVITY LEVEL 1	☐ PROJECT ☒ CONTINUING ACTIVITY	RANK 6

TITLE Maintain Systems Control Program

MANPOWER LOADING			SUPPORT LEVEL			NEW/REVISED STANDARD REQUIRED?	ESTIMATED START DATE	ESTIMATED END DATE
GRADE LEVEL	MANDAYS	40 HR UNITS	AT	ABOVE	BELOW			
35	400	2	☒	☐	☐	☐	1-1-78	12-31-78
			CURRENT LEVEL					

COST ESTIMATE	SAVINGS ESTIMATE	RETURN ON INVESTMENT	RESPONSIBILITIES
STAFF $	STAFF $	ROI% ____	DEPT. ____ ____ ____
HARDWARE	OVERHEAD	YEARS ____	RESP. ____ ____ ____
SOFTWARE	OTHER		
OTHER ____	____		
TOTAL $	TOTAL $		

DESCRIPTION OF ACTIVITY	DESIRED RESULTS/OBJECTIVES
Support the MVS Operating System	Maintain operability

ADVANTAGES OF PERFORMING ACTIVITY	DISADVANTAGES OF PERFORMING ACTIVITY
Maintenance of an operational system	Continued cost of staff expertise

ALTERNATIVE APPROACHES	CONSEQUENCED IF NOT PERFORMED
Convert to VM	System will cease to function.

DEPENDENCIES	APPROVALS
ACTIVITIES ☐ ☐ ☐	PREPARER ____
	DIRECTOR MIS ____
EXTERNAL	DATE PREPARED/REVISED 7/1/78

Exhibit 3.12. Maintain systems control program (Management Information Services).

DECISION PACKAGE

ACTIVITY NAME: Systems Production Control Department DATE: 04/08/80

ASSISTANT V.P.: Chen

EFFORT LEVEL: 1 of 3 RANK: 6

THIS LEVLE IS: Above the current level of effort

DESCRIPTION OF ACTIVITY

This activity monitors completion of all systems jobs including batch header cards, production, merges, and reruns. It also develops and maintains various quality control logs, and various manual and block controls. Additional responsibility is to maintain production library including documentation standardization and distribution.

OBJECTIVE OF ACTIVITY

To insure accurate and comprehensive output for policy recording and financial reporting purposes in life insurance company. This will also define the responsibilities and procedures for controlling the creation and maintenance of all the systems files.

MEASURES OF PERFORMANCE

Direct measures include: (1) Increased accountability for resources used: human, machine/ equipment, and supplies. (2) Increased accountability for time/cost.

This activity will allow us to maintain quality control reports, coordinate outside keypunching service bureau, and handle complaints, problems, and questions from Input/Output control. Having a Systems Production Control Department would create a more cohesive and overall more effective system within the company.

CONSEQUENCES OF NOT FUNDING

Besides the loss of benefits as described above, there will be an increase in the probability of incompetion of systems jobs, increased effort and costs due to lacking of quality control reports, and being lack of integrity and reliability of the whole system.

PROJECTED REVENUES AND/OP COSTS

Annual salary: Systems Production Control Analyst (2)	$36,000
Clerical staff: (5)	45,000
Other costs:	3,000
	$84,000

Costs include on two Systems Production Control Analysts, five clerical persons and specific cost attributable to this function.

ALTERNATIVE APPROACHES

In order to identify and implement a series of processing controls to insure the integrity and reliability of the sytem, there are no other alternates which can substitute this activity. Therefore, an overall framework of organizational and procedural controls must be designed and implemented.

Exhibit 3.13. Systems production control (X Company).

DECISION PACKAGE

DEPARTMENT: Config. Management ACTIVITY: VSAM Support

MANAGER: W. T. Lin LEVEL: 1 RANK: 6

MANPOWER LEVEL: L33-.04 PERSONS, PRODUCT CLASS: ______

TYPE OF EXPERTISE: L33-DASM Analyst

AT X ABOVE ______ BELOW ______ CURRENT LEVEL COST: $1512

DESIRED RESULTS (OBJECTIVES):

Provide mandatory essential level of support for user VSAM data sets

DESCRIPTION OF ACTIVITY:

Respond to user requests for changes to VSAM data set structure

RESPONSIBILITY: (USE LDI CODING)

APP PGM	CONF MGMT	PROD SUPP	TECH SUPP	AFFIL.	
/	IP / CR	/	/	I / P	/

HOW AND WHEN ACCOMPLISHED:

On-going activity, based on user need to establish new VSAM data sets

DEPENDENCIES:

None

ALTERNATIVE APPROACHES:

Same function could be moved elsewhere in the organization, but it would still have to be provided

ADVANTAGES OF RETAINING ACTIVITY:

No choice

DISADVANTAGES:

None

CONSEQUENCES IF ACTIVITY IS ELIMINATED:

A minimal level of VSAM data set administration support must be provided centrally due to the architecture of VSAM

APPROVED BY: ______ DATE: ______

Exhibit 3.14. VSAM support (Y Company).

DECISION PACKAGE

DEPARTMENT: Appl. Programming ACTIVITY: Data Manager Support

MANAGER: T.J. Francl LEVEL: 1 RANK: 20

MANPOWER LEVEL: .05 PERSONS, PRODUCT CLASS: ________

TYPE OF EXPERTISE: 34 Sr. Prog.

AT ______ ABOVE X BELOW ______ CURRENT LEVEL COST: $2,050

DESIRED RESULTS (OBJECTIVES):

Assist TA companies
Maintain centralized control of package maintenance

DESCRIPTION OF ACTIVITY:

Provide caretaker functions for vendor software. Act as primary contact with the vendor and distribute information.

RESPONSIBILITY: (USE LDI CODING)

APP PGM	CONF MGMT	PROD SUPP	TECH SUPP		
I / D	/	/	/	/	/

HOW AND WHEN ACCOMPLISHED:

On going activity

DEPENDENCIES:

None

ALTERNATIVE APPROACHES:

Let another company provide this common function.

ADVANTAGES OF RETAINING ACTIVITY:

Fulfill our charter of centralized maintenance of common system software.

DISADVANTAGES:

None

CONSEQUENCES IF ACTIVITY IS ELIMINATED:

Uncontrolled environment because other companies are not experienced with common systems. Reduced TIS influence in the data processing community.

APPROVED BY: ________________ DATE: ________

Exhibit 3.15. Data manager support (Y Company).

DECISION PACKAGE

DEPARTMENT: Technical Support ACTIVITY: Data Comm. CICS Support

MANAGER: M. A. Vasarhelyi LEVEL: 2 RANK: ______

MANPOWER LEVEL: .25 PERSONS, PRODUCT CLASS: ______

TYPE OF EXPERTISE: (35) Data Comm. Analyst

AT X ABOVE ____ BELOW ____ CURRENT LEVEL COST: $12,000

DESIRED RESULTS (OBJECTIVES):

Assist TA companies

DESCRIPTION OF ACTIVITY:

Evaluate, order, coordinate installation/testing of CICS terminals, lines, modems, TPNS facilities, etc.

RESPONSIBILITY: (USE LDI CODING)

APP PGM	CONF MGMT	PROD SUPP	TECH SUPP	AFFIL.	
/	/	/	P / D	I / CR	/

HOW AND WHEN ACCOMPLISHED:

On-going (based upon user requirements)

DEPENDENCIES:

ALTERNATIVE APPROACHES:

User would place orders themselves (not good)

ADVANTAGES OF RETAINING ACTIVITY:

Provides service to users, centralized control over order and installation of equipment awareness of value system growth

DISADVANTAGES:

CONSEQUENCES IF ACTIVITY IS ELIMINATED:

Users ordering equipment without our knowledge, lack of centralized control

APPROVED BY: ______ DATE: ______

Exhibit 3.16. Data communications support (Y Company).

4
Project Ranking

Setting priorities for decision packages is probably more difficult than actually completing them – not in terms of time spent but in the number of decisions required and the political pressures involved. The ranking process should include decisions by four different management levels within the organization in order to assure responsiveness to the company's needs and to insulate the MIS director from being caught in the middle of highly political situations.

This chapter discusses the criteria for ranking and the ranking process. The first part of the chapter describes the three most common ranking approaches, that is, the single criterion approach, the voting system, and the multiple criteria approach. The second part discusses the ranking process in terms of the four levels of the organizational hierarchy. The four levels of management involved in the ranking process include the first-level MIS department managers who are responsible for the actual completion of the packages, a committee of high-level MIS managers, a user management review committee, and, finally, an executive review board.

CRITERIA FOR RANKING

There are three common ranking approaches: (1) the single criterion approach, (2) the voting system, and (3) the multiple criteria approach. The ranking approach selected should be adapted to the individual organizational needs. The following are descriptions of the three popular approaches.

Single Criterion Approach

This method is the simplest and most appropriate to data processing projects. All projects are evaluated by a single criterion. Examples of the criterion include return on investment (ROI), net present value, cost savings, payback, period, discounted cash flow, or cost-benefit ratio.

Voting System

Oftentimes when it is difficult for the ranking committee to agree on a particular single criterion, a voting system can be used to resolve the disagreement. There are two mechanisms for voting on individual decision packages: (1) Each committee member gets one vote on a fixed scale with either the average or the total points determining the ranking and (2) each committee member gets one vote for each of several criteria with the total points used to determine the ranking.

Multiple Criteria Approach

Logan M. Cheek (1977) suggested the use of five criteria to rank decision packages: (1) Is the activity legally required? (2) Do we have the necessary technical skills? (3) Will line management accept and execute the activity? (4) Will the activity be cost-effective? (5) Can we afford not to select the activity?

RANKING PROCESS

The ranking process provides MIS management with a technique to allocate budget resources. The hierarchy of the ranking process starts at the bottom level, the decision package preparer. It then goes up to the MIS Management Committee, and the User Advisory Committee for second- and third-level review. It finally goes to the MIS Steering Committee for review and final ranking.

1. The Package Preparer

The first ranking should be accomplished by the individual decision unit manager who is responsible for a set of activities and who prepared the associated decision packages. This person is most familiar with the intricate details of each activity and the amount of effort required by each. Because the priority-setting process is based upon the company's needs as a whole rather than individual departmental needs, this manager should be cautioned to take a look at the big picture, rather than just what he is individually responsible for. In those instances where the manager may not fully appreciate the need for recommending a given activity, he should consult with the activity's sponsor for help. This conference may already have taken place when the packages were originally prepared.

An example of a priority scale or range of numbers assigned to each activity is shown in Figure 4.1. Activities with a rank of 1, 2, or 3 are not recommended to be undertaken at this time whereas those with a 4, 5, or 6 carry the individual's recommendation to begin the project or to continue it as in the past.

Priority 1 is assigned to those activities that provide little or no benefit to the company or those that cannot be otherwise justified. These activities are remotely beneficial and will probably never be worked on but have been identified to stimulate thought. Perhaps they will have a better chance next year or may be given a higher priority by succeeding ranking committees.

Priority 2 activities are not much better than priority 1 activities but there is some glimmer of hope that with a greatly expanded staff these items will be considered.

Priority 3 items are those activities that could be justified with increased staff and/or increased resources. The justification to undertake these projects is valid but requires a greater monetary commitment from division management in the form of an expanded MIS budget. For example, if net income exceeds plan by 10%,

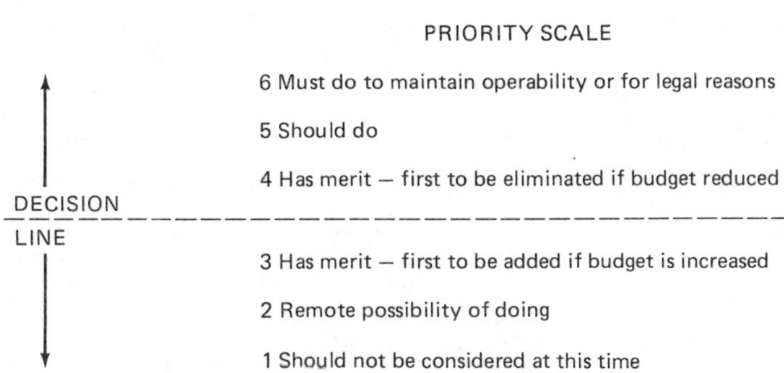

Figure 4.1. Priority scale.

perhaps a few of these activities could be undertaken within the current fiscal year even though they were not originally approved.

Priority 4 activities are quite similar to priority 3 activities except that they have a higher payback or higher degree of preference by the end user. The justification of the activity is still marginal and, if budgets are cut for any reason, these activities would be the first ones to be dropped.

Priority 5 activities are those that are fully justified and will provide a substantial payback to the company in terms of dollars or other tangible and intangible benefits. These items will be completed unless a really significant budget cutback occurs.

Priority 6 activities must be accomplished for overriding reasons including government regulations, contractual agreements, or viability of the company. For example, a payroll system covering 10,000 employees must be supported by programming services because of changes in the tax tables and other user requirements. The company would be out of business if it could not pay its employees on time. It is also unrealistic to operate such a large payroll system manually with a hoard of clerks and unprofitable to hire a service bureau.

Figure 4.2 presents a sample ranking summary form. The following is a list of contents of this sample form:

Date: This is the date prepared by the initiating supervisor or manager.

Department: This is the name of the organizational unit responsible for preparing the associated decision packages.

Prepared: The individual who prepared the summary form if other than the approving supervisor or manager.

Approved: The supervisor or manager approving the rankings shown.

Priority rank: A number from 1 to 6 that specifies the priority assigned to this decision package. The first entry should be the highest level of the priority rank.

Activity number: A number that uniquely identifies this activity.

ZERO-BASE BUDGETING
RANKING SUMMARY

DATE ______ PREPARED ______ PAGE ______

DEPARTMENT ______ APPROVED ______ OF ______

PRIORITY RANK	ACTIVITY NUMBER	NAME	MANPOWER	COST	SAVINGS	RETURN ON INVESTMENT

Figure 4.2. Ranking summary form.

Name: The title of the activity.

Manpower: This section identifies the personnel levels of man-hours obtained from each decision package.

Cost: Expenditure amounts contained in the decision package.

Savings: The benefits to be derived from each activity.

Return on investment: The ROI percentage or payback years obtained from each decision package.

The result of your ranking should now be balanced to the current budgeted headcount and dollars. Chapter 5 contains a detailed discussion about this process. The budget for next year is generated by summing all priority 4, 5, and 6 activities by grade level, rounding wherever necessary.

2. MIS Management Committee

The next level of ranking should be accomplished by higher levels of managers within the Management Information Services Department. Large MIS organizations may find the need to form several such committees to ensure participation by all concerned. The final priority-setting meeting at which the ranking is accomplished should be chaired by the MIS manager and should be attended by his senior management team. Typically, if this number exceeds six people, the meeting will take weeks instead of a day or two. The task of this committee is to confirm or modify the priorities assigned by the individual unit manager. Senior MIS management must review all activities within the department to provide a cross-validation of the initial rankings and to provide a unified stand for the department. Utilizing the concept of participative management, these senior managers have a great deal to say regarding the direction and the efforts to be undertaken by the entire MIS department. Unilateral decisions by the MIS manager can be rejected by later reviews much easier than those that are reached by consensus.

The process of ranking the activities of the department can be extremely time consuming and fraught with personal feelings and salesmanship. Each manager will naturally fight for a larger piece of the total MIS budget. The MIS manager may have to act like a referee to control the meeting so that it can proceed with the task at hand. Try to approach this ranking process with a professional, business-like attitude.

In order to facilitate the ranking process, it is recommended that a cork board (or its equivalent) be secured and blank IBM or index cards be prepared for each activity. The activity number and title should be written on the blank side of the card. The cork board must be quite large and should be able to display most, if not all, of the activities for a given section of the MIS department. Six columns should be established and identified with cards. The labeling will correspond with the six priority categories:

Priority 6 – Essential

Priority 5 – Should do

Priority 4 – Has merit

Priority 3 – Maybe

Priority 2 – Hopeful

Priority 1 – Should not do

As each activity is presented to the committee by the responsible manager, the committee decides which category it should reside in. If the responsible manager disagrees with the committee's ranking, he should lobby for the ranking that his first-line manager chose originally. After agreement, the card is placed under the appropriate heading until all activities have been ranked.

Generally, there is little controversy with those activities that should be considered essential or a high priority. Likewise, there is little controversy with those low-priority items ranked 1 or 2. The critical priorities are those in the middle two categories. Typically these activities are marginally acceptable depending upon the level of funding provided the department. Because the budget line may be raised or lowered subsequent to the ranking process, it is suggested that these activities be ranked sequentially in order of preference within each rank.

Beginning with priority 4 activities, clear the cork board of all other cards including the headings. Select one activity card and pin it to the board. Choosing a second card, hold it aloft next to the first card and ask the question: "Let us assume that there are funds in the coming year for only one of these two activities. Which one shall it be?" Discussion by the committee members is encouraged as long as the big picture and overall MIS objectives are kept in mind. After a decision is made, place the second card above (if superior) or below (if inferior) to the first card. Continue the process with the third activity comparing it to the other two. Compare it to the top-rated activity first and, if it is inferior, compare it to the second-rated activity. Place the third card in the appropriate sequence. Continue this process with the remaining priority 4 activities until all have been sequentially rated. In exactly the same way, sequence the priority 3 activities.

After all priority 3 and 4 activities have been sequenced, record the results for future reference. Prepare a record of the meeting and update the activity packages with any priority changes.

3. User Advisory Committee

Many data processing activities require a substantial amount of resources. Whenever an activity is sponsored by one user department, it usually means that some other sponsor must wait to have its work started. The decision regarding the importance of these activities with respect to one another must be made by the operating managers responsible for several functional areas and for the ultimate success or failure of a group of activities. The burden of priority setting belongs to the end users rather than MIS management. Unless you are the owner of the company and rule with an iron fist or have unlimited resources, let your customers decide what projects or continuing activities will be worked on. For this purpose, the User Advisory Committee (UAC) should be established.

The membership of the UAC should include department/division-level managers that utilize your MIS facility. These individuals are responsible for multiple functional areas and have other managers reporting to them. They sometimes carry the title of director or even vice president but are not upper-level management which would include senior vice presidents. If yours is a very large, multi-divisional company that would result in a large unwieldy committee if all divisional managers were assembled, consider the creation of two or more committees, perhaps along product or geographical lines. These individual committees would then consider only their own activities.

The MIS manager is a member of the advisory committee and, even though he will run the meeting, he is not the chairman. The committee chairman must be chosen from the user community because the role implies superiority. The MIS manager must act as advisor, interrogator, and salesman, not the leader. He prepares the meeting agenda, distributes activity packages, and runs the priority-setting process. The chairman schedules the meeting and ensures that it runs in an orderly manner.

At the first meeting of the User Advisory Committee, a brief presentation should be made about zero base budgeting and the ranking process. It should be emphasized that ZBB is merely a methodology that enhances the decision-making process and contains no inherent magic. A schedule of the key steps in the ZBB preparation process should be discussed and agreed on. The ranking process cannot drag on forever because it is to be used to prepare your budgets next year. In fact, the committee members will utilize the same activity list to prepare their budgets.

Provide each committee member with an *activity catalog* which includes a copy of every decision package to be discussed that day and several reports listing the activities by sponsor, cost, and no forth. See Chapter 7 for examples. Include the results of the MIS department's priority-setting process as a starting point.

The actual ranking process is exactly the same as the one used by the MIS management team. Post all of the IBM cards on a cork board according to their assigned priority. Taking each ranking, the MIS manager and the sponsoring user manager briefly describe each activity. Members are relegated to concurring with the assigned rankings at this time. If the committee decides to modify the priority of any activity, understand why it is changed. Why do they see the situation differently than you and your managers saw it?

Ranking priority 3 and 4 packages is the most difficult part of the meeting and should probably be saved until the other four categories have been completed. Utilize the same sequencing process as before with the MIS management rating as a starting point. Arrange the activity cards on the cork board in the proper order. Taking the highest activity card and holding it next to the card just under it, ask the question: "Assuming that there are only enough funds during the coming year to fund one of these two activities, which one shall it be?" Continue the ranking process as before. Do not be too concerned if the order of the activities changes slightly, but be wary if significant changes are suggested. If you feel strongly enough, lobby for the original ranking along with the responsible operating manager.

Most people have the initial reaction that this User Advisory Committee will not accomplish anything because of the fighting and bickering that will take place. The assumption is made that each manager is self-centered and will fight only for his own projects at the expense of the other groups. On the contrary, these meetings are quite productive, especially if first-line managers are not invited. The participants tend to view the big picture and will compromise their own initial objectives if necessary. It is a real eye-opening experience. The key to the ranking process is to keep the overall objectives of the company in the foreground.

After this meeting, update the activity catalog with any changes. Modifications to various descriptive data elements and their respective priorities may need to be made. Produce a new catalog and a fresh set of reports for each member of the committee and each of your managers.

4. MIS Steering Committee

The establishment of final priorities will be made by the MIS Steering Committee (see Chapter 6) comprised of the highest levels of management, including the chief operating officer. There are two primary reasons why this level of management must be involved in the priority-setting process. Large projects involve tens of thousands of dollars and might even be capitalized. There is no real difference between a systems development project that costs $100,000 and a new furnace or trailer truck. Secondly, they can act as referees in those situations where their subordinates are in conflict with one another over whether or not to grant approval to various projects.

In the first case, it is usually the policy of most corporations that any expenditure over a certain amount must be approved by increasingly higher levels of management. The MIS Steering Committee is an excellent forum for the review of such projects. In many cases, projects can be ranked very high and eventually be approved even though the chief executive is not entirely sold on the idea.

As with the User Advisory Committee, provide each member of the steering committee with an activity catalog. Segregate the large activities and place them in the front of the book. Providing a complete package might be overpowering; if so, make only a few complete activity catalogues available for reference and distribute copies of the larger activities.

In the handouts, include appropriate reports that itemize each activity (see Chapter 7). These reports must list the priority rankings of the UAC and an analysis of projected MIS expenditures required to satisfy priority 4, 5, and 6 activities since this committee is being requested to approve a certain MIS service level whether it is higher or lower than the present level. Reporting each division's expenditure level at this time will eliminate most of the budgetary approval problems in the weeks to come. If a committee member does not wish to spend that much money next year, he is expected to voluntarily lower the rank of his own activity to priority 3 or lower. This is the key to the entire process. For example, if the vice president of Finance cannot afford a new general ledger system and elects to lower its priority, it is better that he make that decision than you. It is no longer necessary for you to delete or postpone projects because of limited staff. The manager of Accounting is not angry at you. He has obviously not demonstrated the real need for a new system to his boss.

Proceed with the project ranking in the same manner as with the User Advisory Committee, but limit the ranking process to only the very large activities. Do not object to using the cork board and IBM cards with this group because it is a flexible and easy to use technique. Rank the large decision packages and, again, do not be concerned about minor changes in priority but be wary of any activities that move from the approved status to the unapproved status or vice versa. Be sure you understand why the change is taking place and the consequences. Do not be afraid to voice your own opinions. You are more than a technical consultant to this group.

After ranking the larger activities, review the smaller activities utilizing a summary report and spend only a small amount of time for each. Do not use the actual decision packages unless greater explanation is required. It may be sufficient to direct committee members' attention to a list of activities for a particular sponsor, allowing them time to review the report and then merely request discussion regarding potential adjustments. It is advisable to avoid analyzing every single activity in detail or even to recite the list.

After agreement on the relative ranking of each activity, the committee's work is essentially complete. An impressive tactic that you can take is to report the results of its decisions back to its members before the meeting is concluded. Have one of your staff members standing by and after the priorities of the larger activities are set, feed him the changes. Repeat this process after the minor activities are covered.

While the data base is being updated and new reports being prepared, discuss another topic such as the remainder of your operational plan. In fact, the entire meeting could be structured around the MIS strategic and operation plans with the ranking process as a subset of the operational plan agenda. Before the meeting is over, distribute the updated reports and request further discussion. Once approved, these activities form the basis for your operational plan and next year's budget. There is no way that your boss can deny you a budget increase or decrease unless he either calls another MIS Steering Committee meeting or is an autocratic majority shareholder.

As with the User Advisory Committee, one might presume that the members of the MIS Steering Committee will fight for their own activities at the expense of the other departments. This is only partially true. If the activities are worth doing, they are worth fighting for. At this level, however managers tend to look at the big picture and beyond their own needs. They are acutely aware of the overall objectives of the corporation and will vote other activities ahead of theirs if they are truly more important.

Another process that will take place during this meeting is the reconciliation between the division/department strategic and operating plans and your MIS plans. They obviously cannot be in conflict if both are to be successfully executed. The controller cannot include a new receivables systems in his plan if the project was not given a sufficiently high priority by the committee. Either the committee's mind must be changed or the controller's plans need to be modified.

An excellent way to employ the MIS Steering Committee whenever economic circumstances demand significant budget cuts during the year is to let them determine what activities should be dropped to priority 3 or lower. Rather than reduce service levels in a vacuum, shift that responsibility to the users. Let them take the heat from their staff for the cancellation of a project.

The entire discussion of activity ranking presumes limited MIS resources and is a waste of time given a completely flexible budget. With unlimited resources, any activity that the users desire will be approved. The burden of finding additional funds rests upon the user, not you.

5
Budget Formulation

This chapter deals with the actual formulation of a data processing budget after the zero base (or traditional) activity selection has been performed. The first part describes a series of basic principles of an organizational nature related to the corporate planning process. Then, the behavioral bases for the organizational budget process are discussed. Among these are motivation, budget standards, participation, and budget slack. The next part of the chapter relates the setting of budgets through the zero base budgeting approach to a more traditional context. Additionally, it relates the advantages of the zero base methodology to key issues in the budget-setting process.

The fifth part describes the budgeting process for the acquisition of hardware, software, and applications. These are presented by illustrative anecdotes. Next, a budget account plan is outlined for potential use by the reader. Finally, key conclusions are drawn and various practical suggestions for managers and other MIS personnel are listed.

ORGANIZATIONAL BUDGETING

This section describes the key features of the budgeting process for a management information services organization. It is essential to emphasize the need to integrate an organization's MIS plans with its corporate plans. We shall start by defining three basic concepts necessary for placing this issue a more general context: planning, forecasting, and budgeting.

Planning

Although a lengthy discussion of strategic planning is included in Chapter 1, a further example is appropriate here. Planning is the process by which the organization looks toward the future, assesses its objectives and potentials, identifies key problems of the current environment, generates alternatives for future action, and chooses between these alternatives to create a scenario for future action.

As an example, let us describe a small organization that sells information services to students who intend to enter a university and would like to obtain a scholarship. This organization, Scholarships International (SI), has been in business for about four years and markets its scholarship search service in a series of selected areas in the United States. Its current operations involve direct mail advertising and receipt of orders through a New York post office box and with a toll-free "800" telephone number.

Once a set of orders is received, a data collection form is key-entered on a CRT connected to a PDP 11/34 computer. The data is edited at the time of entry and accumulated for a later batch run. The computer programs that process the data is kept in alpha-numeric form using sequential access methods. Figure 5.1 displays the characteristics of the system in general terms.

The computer is used on a time-sharing basis at the cost of \$10.00 per hour of connect time. No charges are made for CPU time but disk space and printed output are charged for. One of the major inconveniences of the service is that for any substantial printing, the batch service and delivery must conform to the computer center's guidelines which are not very responsive to SI's needs. Over the last three years, SI spent \$17,000, \$19,500, and \$25,000, respectively, for computer processing.

Management is planning for future data processing needs and is attempting to decide on alternatives.

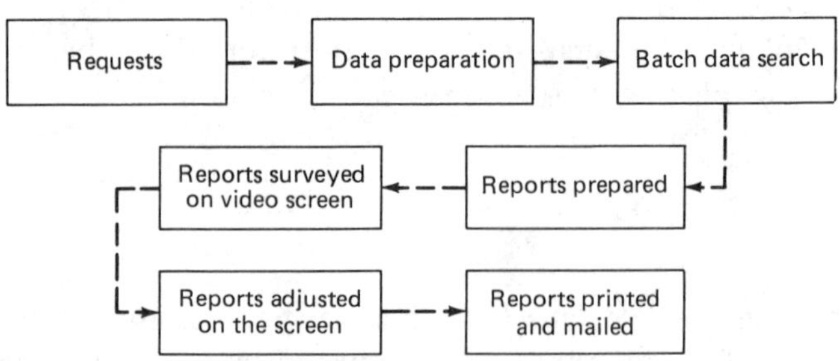

Figure 5.1. SI system description.

Objective

The primary objective of SI is to have the best possible quality of scholarship information services for the least possible cost while maintaining a specified minimum level of reliability.

Problem Formulation

The problems faced by SI involve the following:

1. Potentially excessive costs
2. Lengthy turnaround time for printouts (delivered once a day)
3. Limited reliability of the system presently in use (goes down several times a day for 10 to 15 minutes each time)

Generating Alternatives

Management has examined the problem and has generated a series of alternatives:

1. Purchase of their own computer
2. Find a new computer service bureau
3. Renegotiate the present service bureau's rates and services
4. Convert the system to operate on multiple microcomputers

Evaluation of Alternatives

A series of parameters of cost and desirability are attributed to each alternative in order to compare and contrast them. These often result from a "best judgment" approach as opposed to a carefully studied alternative.

Alternative Choice

After a consideration of the system's objectives, a choice is made among the four alternatives stated above.

FORECASTING

The process of planning described above is supplemented by a prediction of the future; a view of what to expect from the environment made by experts. Two types of forecasts may be related here: global forecasts and conditional forecasts.

Global forecasts indicate changes and conditions in the environment independent of actions by the planning entity. In the example above, SI would utilize global forecasts to estimate the expected college enrollment, financial aid needs, demographics, and so on. Meanwhile, conditional forecasts are previsions of the state of the world as modified by certain actions of the planning entity. For example, if SI spends $300,000 in advertising, what will be the expected number of scholarship report inquiries, requests, and the resulting market share?

Forecasting is an entire field unto itself. It has been divided into three main types of methodologies by Chambers, Mullick, and Smith (1971) which are: qualitative techniques, time series analysis and projection, and causal models. Forecasting also tends to be focused very quantitatively. The reader may use Markidakis and Wheelwright (1978) to acquire further knowledge of the subject.

As an illustration of forecasting in the modern corporate world, continuing with the SI example, Exhibit 5.1 in this chapter's appendix shows SI's utilization of a popular spread sheet software to use linear regression in order to predict the market for its scholarship information product. SUPERCALC is demonstrated but other products such as VISICALC, AUTOTAB, and FORESIGHT work equally well.

BUDGETING

There are two types of budgets that are interrelated in their utilization: operating budgets and capital budgets. The operating budget takes into account the projected workload and the resources needed to service these workload levels. The capital expenditure budget relates to major expense items and reflects strategic decisions by the firm.

Capital expenditures (i.e., the construction of a new computer center) are reflected in the operating budgets of the center with advanced chargeout schemes. This is done through depreciation of other fixed-cost allocation-type charges.

Data center revenues are difficult to forecast because they suffer the same problems of chargeout schemes. They will be discussed in Chapters 6 and 8. Fixed incomes come from corporate allocations and contract income. Variable incomes come from internal and external users of EDP services.

Budgeting is the numerical and detailed quantification of the final results of the planning process for a relatively short time frame (usually one year). Five- and ten-year plans (as well as strategic plans) usually have general numbers associated with them without a great level of detail or breakdown. Plans entail sufficient data to make optimization decisions but are not specific enough for control purposes. Consequently, a series of detailed budgets must serve as an implementation guide for the control effort. Figure 5.2 provides an illustration of the level of detail that will be encompassed in the

		Totals
A. One-time expenses		
Hardware acquisition		
Mainframe	$ 32,000	
Peripherals	23,000	55,000
Software acquisition		
Internat. bank.	120,000	
Word processing	1,500	
Other miscell.	5,000	126,500
Personnel training		
User courses	3,000	
Management	5,000	
Consultants	5,000	13,000
Installation costs		
Physical facility	9,000	
Consulting	10,000	
Other	5,000	24,000
Forms and supplies		
Miscellaneous	5,000	5,000
		$223,500
B. Monthly costs		
Hardware maintenance	517	
Software (OS) mainten.	259	
Banking software mainten.	800	
Supplies	600	
Personnel (2 persons)	2,000	
Miscellaneous	500	
		$4,676

Figure 5.2. Preliminary MIS expense budget Bank of another country.

preliminary expense budget for the acquisition of a data processing facility by a small foreign bank's branch in New York.

In order to obtain a more comprehensive understanding of the role, philosophy, and objectives of budgeting, we must first talk about the concept and the organization of responsibility centers. In the modern world of management, organizations must be subdivided into organic units that are managed as semi-autonomous entities. With their increased size and complexity, these entities have to be planned, controlled, and evaluated in relation to some organizational scheme, such as:

1. *Cost centers:* responsibility centers that are evaluated in terms of the costs they incur. Optimally they should be evaluated in terms of *controllable* costs or costs that management has discretion over. Unfortunately, in practice, a segregation between controllable and noncontrollable costs is difficult to make and depends to a certain extent on the time frame of the decision. Often the smaller, lower-level responsibility centers tend to be cost centers with no direct revenue of their own.
2. *Profit centers:* a responsibility center where there are costs and revenues leading to a degree of controllability of profits. In for-profit organizations, these tend to operate better and be more in focus with organizational objectives. Later in this chapter we will discuss how profit centers may increase goal congruence.
3. *Investment centers:* a responsibility center that focuses on the relationship between profits and the assets employed in earning them. The return on investment of these centers is carefully measured and monitored.

The nature and emphasis of these different types of responsibility centers leads to substantially different divisional and subcorporate responses which need to be examined in order to understand their behavioral implications.

BEHAVIORAL IMPLICATIONS

The main essence of budgets with a framework of profit planning, management, and control is their behavioral implications. Going back to essentials, if owners and managers (who are agents of the owners) did not believe that budgets (1) increase the long-term profitability of the business, (2) decrease the risk of doing business, (3) improve the mechanics of the agent/owner relationship, or (4) any combination of the above, organizations would not adopt budgeting systems. Therefore, if a large number of U.S. organizations have budget systems, it is obvious that they are cost beneficial and that these budgets must affect organizations primarily by their behavioral and control features. We shall further explore behavioral characteristics and cover budgetary control later in this chapter and in Chapter 6.

Expectancy theory (Ronen and Livingstone 1975) basically explains human motivation in terms of personal satisfaction relative to a task and satisfaction with the rewards of a task as potentially received and perceived by the person. A modified expectancy motivation equation could be expressed as:

$$M = IV_b + P_1 \; IV_a + \sum_{i\text{-}1} P_{2i} \times EV_i$$

where

M = motivation to work
P_1 = probability that hard work toward the objective will enable the goal to be achieved
IV_a = internal satisfaction related to achieving successfully the task
IV_b = internal satisfaction with having a goal to work toward
P_{2i} = the probability that achieving the goal will lead to reward i (i.e., salary increase, promotion, etc.)
EV_i = satisfaction with obtaining reward i.

This means that motivation is a result of the satisfaction of having a goal added to the probability that effort toward the goal will result in its achievement multiplied by the satisfaction of achieving that goal added to the summation of all potential rewards weighted by the probability of achieving a reward.

For example, the motivation of a team project leader can be posited as the sum of two main elements:

1. His satisfaction in having the task to perform.

2. The probability that increased effort will improve the task performance expectation multiplied by the total satisfaction that comes from the achievement of the task. This total satisfaction, in turn, is composed of two elements: (a) satisfaction with successful achievement of the task and (b) summation of composite reward satisfaction, for example, the probability of promotion multipled by the satisfaction provided by promotion plus the probability of increased peer respect multiplied by its satisfaction, and so on.

Using the above model, Ronen and Livingstone proceed to support what they call "five general assumptions made in accounting with respect to budgets and behavior." We shall discuss these assumptions in general terms:

1. Budget standards should be reasonably attainable. This requirement helps to determine the level at which budget standards should be set. *Engineering* (or optimal) standards are very high and make no concessions to the human nature of socio-technical systems. *Laissez-faire* standards are set at easily attainable levels which do not improve or press upon productivity. Some labor contracts set standards of this type and resist management efforts to raise productivity. *Reasonably attainable* standards are somewhat above the normally achievable level.

2. Participation in the budget process leads to better performance. When workers are involved in the process of setting budgets, they will then try harder to make them realistic. In software development projects, it is highly desirable to involve project leaders, participants, managers, and users when setting up decision packages or project budgets. Of particular consideration to DP-type budgeting is the need to harmonize production and development costs in a common framework. Though this is often difficult to do, some financial tools such as present-value accounting and annuities may serve to integrate activities that appear as different as the proverbial apples and oranges.

For example, two groups in a project development team are arguing for substantially different levels of efficiency and effectiveness in a system. The first group will develop its own search algorithms for maximum efficiency at a development cost of $200,000 and a monthly operating cost of $2,500.

The second faction will use "brute force" in its approach, leading to the same reports but at a greatly reduced level of programming effort. The development cost is estimated to be \$160,000 and operating costs are \$5,000 a month.

Assuming a 1% monthly incremental borrowing rate and a 5 year life expectancy for the application with no residual software value, we perform the following calculations:

Team 1:
200,000 + present value of an annuity of \$2,500 for 5 years at 12%
= 200,000 + 2,500 × 3.604
= 209,010

Team 2:
160,000 + present value of an annuity of \$5,000 for 5 years at 12%
= 160,000 + 5,000 × 3.604
= 178,020

which leads us to the choice of alternative 2.

3. Management by exception is effective. One application of this concept is the use of steering committees in data processing organizations (see Chapter 6) where planning and control are based on budgets and remedial action is based on budget discrepancies.

4. Noncontrollable items should be excluded from budget reports. As we discussed earlier, a manager's motivation is a direct function of his individual ability to affect the outcome of the responsibility center. Therefore, the DP manager should be held accountable only for the things over which he can exert control.

As mentioned earlier, this is easier said than done and, despite its being an attractive principle, it is relatively difficult to implement. For example, should the DP manager be charged with the depreciation of equipment previously purchased? The argument for this policy would be that if he was instrumental in acquiring the system, it is a valid charge. The opposing argument would be that if it was corporate policy to acquire the equipment, then the manager is bound by a decision he might have avoided by renting.

5. Budgetary accounting should be restricted to criteria measurable in monetary terms. Unless measurement is adequate and reasonably accurate, the budget substantially loses its purpose.

GOAL ORIENTATION

Another behavioral factor that must be discussed is goal orientation. Budgets produce the distinctive effect of forcing organizational goals to be openly stated and uniformly followed. Goal consonance means that the entire organization endeavors to reach similar goals. On the other hand, a poorly tuned profit center system may generate organizational goal dissonance which implies that subunit efforts may even be counter-effective.

Budget slack is a factor characteristic of managers responsible for divisional performance. They pool their estimate of resources needed for maintaining flexibility in their management action. Such behavior is not necessarily disfunctional, but rather a recognition of the fact that managers cannot perfectly predict the world at budget time.

How is slack introduced into the budget? Every year the DP manager of a certain major university would include a software acquisition cost in his budget that he did not intend to use. Later in the year he would transfer the funds to accounts where there was a real need. Similar techniques abound throughout the business world.

THE TRADITIONAL BUDGET

Once organizational plans are set, they are transformed into operating budgets on a multi-annual or annual basis. Budgets tend to be set up using either a *bottom-up* or a *top-down* method.

The bottom-up method usually has responsibility centers proposing certain levels of revenue and corresponding levels of expense. These are submitted to successive levels of the organization up to the top budget officer who examines the individual and global figures and suggests adjustments. On the other hand, in the top-down approach top management initiates and imposes budgets. A more common approach is a top management budget guideline that is issued between six and eight months prior to the beginning of the fiscal year to which responsibility centers respond by preparing budgets and/or filing for exemptions or discrepancies from the guidelines through budget justification methods.

Traditional budgets tend to rely heavily on historical results for establishing new levels of revenue and expense. The most common way to set a budget is to get the last year's figures and add to them a certain percentage (e.g., 10%). This method is an anathema to the concept of zero base budgeting that is discussed and presented throughout this book.

In a DP entity – which may be a separately organized company, a division of a larger organization, or a service center that provides internal and external services – we find certain specific problems that should be discussed. In its annual meeting, the steering committee should set up general guidelines for the MIS budget in which capital and operating expenses are identified and separated. Such figures may be related to a proposed profit center revenue estimate that was provided by MIS management.

For example, let us consider the MIS department of a small to medium-sized manufacturing operation located in Illinois. The company contracts for and manufactures sheets and curtains for wholesale marketing. They are currently running an IBM System 3 that was purchased six years ago and was depreciated over eight years using a simple straight-line method.

Figure 5.3 presents the department's budget in an abbreviated form. The MIS manager does all of the department's analysis and programming himself. He has his hands full keeping the system working and therefore has little time to enhance it or to develop new systems.

A traditional budgeting procedure would establish a budget for the MIS department in 1983 of $151,800, an increase of 10%. This procedure, which reflects a top-down across-the-board budget allocation, does not take the following points into consideration:

Personnel expenses		
DP manager	$32,000	
Operator	18,000	
Key entry person	16,000	
Social costs	22,000	
		$88,000
Preprinted forms and supplies		10,000
Hardware maintenance		22,000
Utilities		8,000
Miscellaneous		10,000
Total Basic Budget		$138,000

Figure 5.3. Summary MIS budget for 1983 (Sheet and Curtain Company).

1. The implicit cost of the machine's depreciation
2. The potential economies (or costs) of replacing the machine with a System 38 or a HP 3000
3. The need for a new payroll system that must be contracted to outside consultants
4. The need of a tape drive for disk backup

On the other hand, a bottom-up approach to budgeting might reflect a myopic, computer-oriented view of the MIS department without an understanding of the organization in its general context. Budget control forms printed by the system might look like Figure 5.4.

The traditional budget control report shown in Figure 5.4 has the typical problem of trying to budget evenly throughout the year for expenses that vary over the year. For example, inventory counts take place in January and tax reporting occurs in March. These activities will use substantially more paper than the other months, which leads to a negative budget variance. The opposite condition, in which a small volume of sales leads to less data preparation hours, would lead to the false impression of budgetary economies or efficiencies.

Finally, there is the problem of budgeting for the new order-control system that corporate offices are so vociferously requesting. In a traditional setting, a new line item for contract software would be added to the budget. The ZBB approach, on the other hand, would

Month of: MARCH — Date: 4/2/82

BUDGET ITEM	YEARLY ALLOCATION	THIS MONTH Bud.	Act.	Var.	CUMMULATIVE Bud.	Act.	Var.
Personnel	88,000	7334	7306	+28	22000	21948	+52
Pre-printed forms/supplies	10,000	834	1065	−231	2500	2940	−440
Hardware Maintainance	22,000	1834	1834	0	5500	5500	0
Utilities	8,000	667	661	+6	2000	1987	+13
Miscellaneous	10,000	834	830	+4	2500	2515	−15

Figure 5.4. Budget control sheet (Sheet and Curtain Company).

require the preparation of decision packages and some evaluation of joint effects.

Traditional budgets have a series of objectives among which are: (1) a quantitative statement of objectives, (2) a way to control performance, (3) a tool of integration among different divisions, and (4) a way to coordinate operations.

In data processing, we can add additional objectives: (5) a tool for communication between top management and MIS management who talk different languages, (6) a mechanism to protect MIS management from excessive political pressure by users, and (7) a tool for choice among competing alternatives in the ZBB setting which is discussed below.

ZBB AND THE BUDGET PROCESS

Previous chapters have already examined the key features of the zero base budgeting process from the design of decision packages to their evaluation and selection. This section attempts to place this process in the context of traditional budgets and the cost control mechanisms described in Chapter 6.

Figure 2.7 described the sequence of events for a ZBB system. We must place this in a more general context not only because of the choice among competing alternatives but also for control of the DP resource. Therefore, let us assume a *bottom-up* planning system that operates with corporate guidelines and a steering committee. The last three steps of Figure 2.7 are encompassed in Figure 5.5 as the process of application selection.

In accordance with corporate guidelines and the organizational strategic plan, the steering committee will issue decision package guidelines. Decision packages will be prepared by the divisions and submitted to the steering committee that will proceed with the ranking and selection procedures. Decision packages that are selected and adjusted will be returned to the divisions for further budget detail and will serve as components for the traditional budgets of the user and MIS departments. The final results will be integrated into an *MIS master plan,* a very important control standard for the organization. In Appendix 2 of this chapter, we suggest general guidelines for preparation of such a master plan.

This master plan is compared with actual performance, the attainment of project milestones, and other data from the corporate management information system so that the steering committee can perform its control functions and can adjust its planning to thus complete the planning/budgeting/control cycle.

The integration of the zero base approach into the traditional budget approach refines the advantageous behavioral features of the process. The zero base approach allows for the annual scrutiny of parts of the organization's budget that under the traditional method would be taken for granted.

This allows for constant goal consistency adjustment year to year for the organization and its divisions. Plans and projects that are no longer in the mainstream of organization objectives may be dropped, deemphasized, or redirected.

The typical criticism of ZBB is the fact that the process is expensive and unnecessary for basic corporate activities. This criticism can be bypassed in an EDP setting by having a basic production budget that is not set up as a decision package every year and that is adjusted by some type of inflation index.

Budgeting in the early stages of data processing, much like traditional budgeting today, tended to fund most of what DP management desired. Stibbens (1982) points out that "in the old days 'machine accounting' managers could crank out next year's budget by merely writing numbers – any numbers – on a piece of paper. Senior management didn't approve these numbers; they acquiesed. Those days are gone forever."

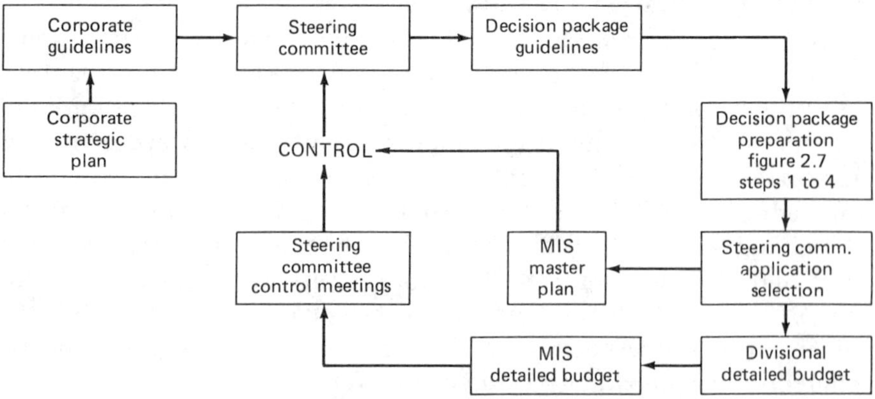

Figure 5.5. The MIS planning/budget/control cycle.

BUDGETS FOR ACQUISITION

When addressing the problems of budgets for operations and for acquisitions, which are similar in nature, it may be desirable to discuss some particularly interesting details. The first general rule in the acquisition of MIS-related items is that it always costs more than it appears at first glance. We shall use a series of anecdotes based on real-life events to illustrate acquisition budgeting problems.

Software Acquisition by Development

A major computer manufacturer developed the operating system for its new line of hardware in-house. This operating software was completed 1.5 years after the scheduled completion date at a cost 250% higher than the original budgeted amount which resulted in major financial losses for the vendor and a flood of lawsuits.

Software development budgeting is very risky and difficult to estimate. Experience and detailed project estimates will help in its formulation.

Software Acquisition by Purchase

The acquisition of preprogrammed software is becoming an increasing portion of MIS budgets with projections that it may account for about 20% of MIS budgets by 1990. In a world of increasing user sophistication and increased complexity of software packages, the problem of evaluation and cost estimation is of prime importance.

A major U.S. bank was establishing a New York office to manage and procure international operations. It wished to benefit from recent regulations allowing the establishment of international banking facilities in New York City. One of the top systems analysts from their corporate offices and a local consultant under contract made contacts with manufacturers and other banks showing a dazzling array of possibilities for preprogrammed software to support international banking operations ranging in cost from \$50,000 to over \$1,000,000. The proposals encompassed a whole range of options from a self-contained system on a microcomputer with limited capabilities to the utilization of an international network of computers based in Canada.

In addition to outright purchase (or lease) costs, there were substantial differences in operations costs, some of which were difficult to estimate. Figure 5.6 illustrates some of the main cost items to be estimated in the acquisition of software.

In addition to the costs described in Figure 5.6, a series of other costs were incurred by the bank as a result of its software acquisition. The first major cost, most often neglected due to its incremental nature, is the cost of the time involved by management in the contract negotiations with the vendor and in the specification, selection, supervision, and implementation of the system. Some authors in the literature suggest costs of up to one third of the original purchase price of the software as the lower boundary of management involvement costs in the acquisition of software. The bank in the anecdote did not budget for these costs because they were considered part of the normal operating costs and because it was assumed that either a manual or an automated system would have to be established. In addition to this major cost item, other smaller costs may also add up, for example, the costs of preprinted forms, utilities, data preparation, technical journals, and other supplies.

As a final note on hidden costs, the IBM System 38 offers the option of a completely integrated management information system. This software would perform most commercial support functions for a business in operation. The complete cost of this option is about twice the cost of the hardware based in terms of monthly lease amounts. A recent study in a consulting engagement for a small

A. Acquisition Costs	
Basic software	$120,000
Source code and docum.	6,000
Additional module	12,000
1st year maintenance	8,000
	$146,000
B. One-Time Costs	
Installation charge	$ 10,000
User training charges	15,000
Consulting charges	12,000
	$ 37,000
C. Monthly Costs	
Software maintenance charge	$ 800

Figure 5.6. Software Acquisition Budget (Bank of another state).

manufacturer indicated that the tradeoffs between development and maintenance or purchase and maintenance by the supplier of this integrated software clearly favor the second alternative by a factor of 2 to 2.5.

Hardware Acquisition Costs

The problem of hardware selection, choice, and acquisition is extensively discussed in many textbooks (for example, Joslin 1968). Nevertheless, total hardware cost estimates are difficult to develop and often result in unrealistic numbers.

A subsidiary of a major European drug manufacturer was established in New York in order to control the import and distribution of wholesale drugs from Europe to the U.S. market. Most of the software necessary for this operation was available from a firm in Hong Kong. All programs were written in a higher-level language compatible to most of the minicomputers on the market. The hardware specifications required a machine with 128K memory and 256MB of disk space, the capability to support up to 16 ports, and the availability of either tape or floppy disk devices.

Bids were requested from several manufacturers including IBM which proposed its System 34. A survey of the bids indicated that for a similar hardware configuration, IBM costs were about 15% higher and had somewhat more expensive monthly maintenance for hardware and operating software. It was also obvious that users rated the quality of IBM systems support significantly higher than the other bid responders. The main elements of system costs were:

Mainframe
Additional ports
Tape drive
Terminals
600 lpm printer
3780 Communications support
Cables and other accessories

In addition to the above, most manufacturers had extra monthly usage charges for its operating system and/or main software and utility components.

Application Selection Budgets

In the previous chapters we discussed decision package completion and the ranking selection process. We shall now discuss, using another anecdote, the problems with decision packages and the numbers that go into their formulation.

A major U.S. company with its corporate offices in Texas has a system of distributed data processing and development and a steering committee that operates out of the corporate office. Management requests incremental decision packages from all operating DP divisions about six months prior to fiscal year end and requests responses in two months. Their ZBB approach dictates that decision packages for expenses above the 80% level are arbitrarily set as a "basic operating budget" and do not have to be justified because of the basic nature and breakdown of expenses. An arbitrary number is used as a decision package threshold where projects of maintenance or minor modification can be performed at the local level without steering committee approval and can be funded out of the basic operating budget. The system seems to work well and the entire planning and software implementation process runs smoothly and effectively. An after-the-fact evaluation of the processes of decision package budget setting revealed a series of interesting facts:

1. Project costs were underestimated consistently by approximately 20 to 30%. On the other hand, project managers thus displayed a consistent ability during budgeting to forecast the cost a project would likely incur.
2. Substantial gaming occurred in the manipulation of decision packages with some packages proposed just for the purpose of being cut, others divided into minor portions to stay away from the steering committee, and substantial negotiation among users for mutual support.

A BUDGET PLAN

Zero base budgeting has been heralded as the solution for a more rational and less painful budget process. Actually it provides highly improved inputs not only for the planning and selection process but also for the *control* process through decision package worksheets that can be aggregated into a report. Figure 5.7 shows a summary of the data flow for this budget control process.

Figure 5.7 illustrates a series of approved decision packages being used as a control device and integrated horizontally into an MIS department control budget. Package variances which may have been unnoticeable at departmental levels are important for project control purposes. This scheme can be easily implemented into an automated system allowing for timely monitoring of project progress. It can be combined with a more complex scheme of data gathering for the key elements of MIS budgets as described in Figure 5.8.

Figure 5.8 can be related to a standard organization *chart of accounts* for MIS budgeting (adapted from "Guidelines for Cost Accounting Practices for Data Processing," *Data Base,* winter 1977 supplement). Let us discuss data gathering associated with the main items of expense.

BASIC MIS BUDGET		
EXPENSE CODE & NAME	BUDGET	ACTUAL
0100 Salaries		
0410 Property taxes		
0460 Employee taxes		
0500 Energy		
0600 Supplies		
0800 Unclassified		
0900 Travel/entertain.		
1000 Communications		
1210 Property insurance		
1260 Employee insurance		
1300 Depreciation		
1700 Equipment rentals		
1930 Test time		

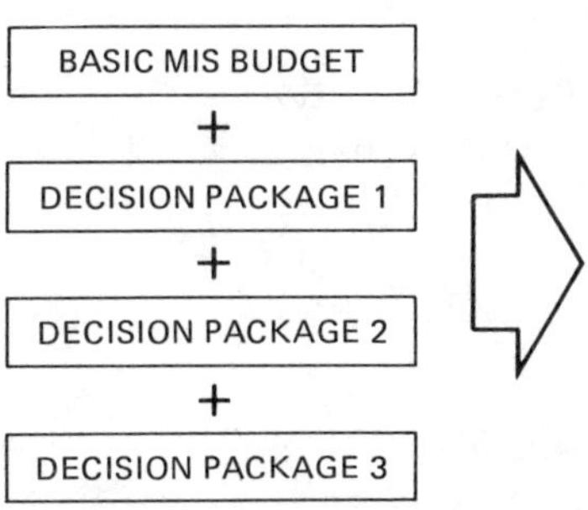

BUDGET CONTROL SHEET		
EXPENSE	BUDGET	ACTUAL
Salaries		
Taxes		
Energy		
Supplies		
Unclassified		
Travel/enter.		
Communicat.		
Insurance		
Depreciation		
•		
•		
•		

Figure 5.7. Decision package integration.

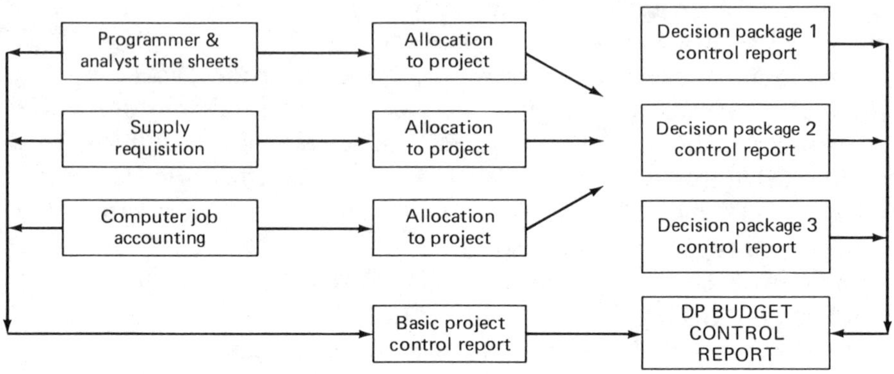

Figure 5.8. Budget data-gathering mechanisms.

Salary and personnel costs gathered from timesheets, time cards, and the payroll system can be broken down into:

1. Base wages
   a. Management
   b. Non-management
2. Part-time work
3. Overtime
4. Benefits
5. Taxes
6. Employment fees
7. Travel
8. Moving expenses
9. Other

Office-space-related costs may be drawn directly from an accounts payable system or from overhead allocation schemes.

1. Rent
2. Electricity
3. Heat
4. Water
5. Taxes, property and personal
6. Depreciation
7. Building improvements
8. Maintenance and repairs

9. Insurance
10. Security services
11. Other

Equipment and related costs are drawn from the same sources as above except that they are easier to allocate to particular projects (decision packages). A system with online accounting and/or job cards that discriminate (1) the user of the hardware (e.g., Peter Simmons, programmer), (2) the department (MIS Programming), (3) the project (payroll tax updates), and (4) the nature (development, integration, operation, auditing) may serve as the primary hardware cost allocation mechanism.

1. Computer hardware
    a. Rent
    b. Lease
    c. Depreciation
    d. Maintenance
2. Office machines
    a. Rent
    b. Lease
    c. Depreciation
    d. Maintenance
3. Application and systems software
    a. Rent
    b. Purchase or lease
    c. Maintenance
4. Insurance
5. Property tax

Communications-related expenses can also be gathered through the accounts payable system. It should be noted that these expenses are often charged directly to user departments and grossly understated in the MIS budget which may cause serious distortions in project control and follow-up. These costs encompass intra- and inter-office lines for data and/or voice communications.

1. Communications hardware
    a. Rent or lease
    b. Depreciation
    c. Maintenance

2. Usage of communication lines
3. Other

Supplies and other expenses include:

1. Tapes
2. Disks and floppy diskettes
3. Card stock
4. Printer ribbons
5. Continuous forms
6. COM film and chemicals
7. Packaging and binding materials
8. Freight
9. Subscriptions and manuals
10. Stationary and office supplies
11. Postage
12. Outside services
13. Consulting services
14. Printing and reproduction
15. Audio/visual services
16. Entertainment
17. Central office overhead
18. Marketing allocation
19. Charges from other departments
20. Other

All of these expense line items can be related to activity types that may be broken down as follows:

1. Systems and programming
   a. Administration
   b. Systems analysis and systems design
   c. Program design and programming
   d. System testing and installation
   e. Post-installation audit
   f. System maintenance
2. Technical support
   a. Administration
   b. Standards

- c. Operating software
- d. Hardware
- e. Assistance and training

3. Data processing operations
    - a. Administration
    - b. Control
        - (1) Data collection
        - (2) Data control
        - (3) Data distribution
        - (4) Quality control
        - (5) Production control
    - c. Offline
        - (1) Data entry
        - (2) Tabulating
        - (3) Teletype
        - (4) Microfilm
    - d. Computer operations
        - (1) Processing
            - (a) Local batch
            - (b) Remote batch
            - (c) Online
            - (d) Time sharing
        - (2) Peripheral
            - (a) Printing
            - (b) Card reading
            - (c) Card punching
            - (d) Scanning
            - (e) Paper tape conversion
            - (f) Plotter
            - (g) Ticket conversion
            - (h) Telecommunications
            - (i) Analog digital
            - (j) Permanent storage

This general account structure, which relates type of expense to activity, can be associated with the different approved (or proposed) decision packages for a complete three dimensional budget plan as shown in Figure 5.9.

	SYSTEMS & PROGRAMMING	TECHNICAL SUPPORT	D.P. OPERATIONS
Salaries			
Occupancy			
Equipment			
Communications			
Supplies			
Other			

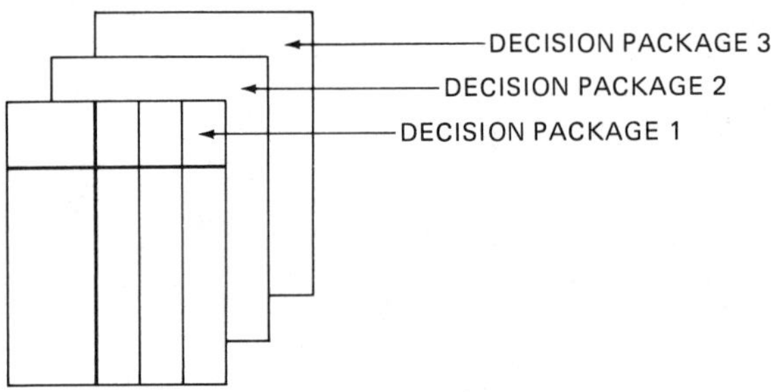

Figure 5.9. A simplified budget plan.

CONCLUSIONS

A general framework for MIS budgeting was presented in this chapter. A budget is an extremely sensitive tool and must be custom-adapted to the organization. The cost characteristics of the different items of expense, to be discussed in Chapter 6, are the principal determinants of the adequacy of the budget control scheme.

Ability to control costs is the principal determinant of the adequacy of budgets as control devices. On the other hand, the planning and budget processes have the intrinsic benefit of forcing a systematic evaluation of the organization's present and future plans in addition to its ability to maintain control.

Zero base budgeting was presented as the preferred device for taking a series of potential activities and aggregating them into a comprehensive MIS plan. This plan was shown to be a good control device and a basic document for the development of the traditional budget plan. Budgets were shown to be fundamentally a behavioral tool for improved corporate performance.

The following recommendations summarize the discussions in this chapter:

- Planning, budgeting, and forecasting are the component processes of the organization's look at the future.
- Budgeting is essentially a behaviorally oriented process to increase responsibility center manager motivation.
- Motivation is a composite of rewards associated with the job and the satisfaction presented by the job itself.
- Budget standards should be set at high but attainable levels with the participation of the budgeters.
- Budgeted items should be easily measurable and controllable.

Appendix 1: Forecasting Example using *SUPERCALC*

The example below illustrates a simplified method that Scholarships International (SI) could use to forecast the demand for scholarship services, applying linear regression to historical data.

```
  |  A    ||   B    ||   C    ||   D    ||   E    ||   F    ||   G   |
 1|CALCULATIONS TO DETERMINE LINEAR REGRESSION EQUATION
 2|
 3|SAMPLE    COLLEGE   SCHOLARSHIP
 4|CITIES    POPULAT.  APPL. REQUEST       P*D       P^2       D^2
 5|          VAR: P    VAR: D
 6|----------------------------------------------------------------------
 7| 1         35640         3948          1.4071e8  1.2702e9  15586704
 8| 2         20870         2528          52759360  4.3556e8  6390784.
 9| 3         15839         2047          32422433  2.5087e8  4190209.
10| 4         5984           941          5630944   35808256  885481.0
11| 5         7448          1325          9868600   55472704  1755625.
12| 6         8760          1630          14278800  76737600  2656900.
13| 7         40800         4695          1.9156e8  1.6646e9  22043025
14| 8         6830           975          6659250   46648900  950625.0
15| 9         9650          1004          9688600   93122500  1008016.
16| 10        6235           894          5574090   38875225  799236.0
17| 11        10250         1106          11336500  1.0506e8  1223236.
18| 12        15200         1345          20444000  2.3104e8  1809025.
19|----------------------------------------------------------------------
20|TOTALS     183506       22438          5.0093e8  4.3040e9  59298866
21|
22|
23|          AVERAGE   AVERAGE #
24|          POPULAT.  REQUESTS
25|
26|           15292.17 1869.833
27|
28|REGRESSION EQUATION
29|
30|D = a + bP
31|
32|                    b=         .1223373
33|
34|a = D-bP= -11.6347
35|
36|Therefore the regression equation for
37|estimating demand of scholarships is:
38|
39|D = -11.63 + .122P
```

Appendix 2: Management Information Services Master Plan

- Define general objectives
- Define operational objectives
- Define global line of the macrosystem (10 years)
- Patterns of applications
- Methods of distributing costs
  Direct overhead
  Partial or total chargeout
- Define macroapplications (integrated focus)
- *Do not:*
  Discuss details about the budget
  Discuss details about the equipment
  Interfere with the personnel

THE FORMAL MIS PLAN – A MODEL

1. Introduction
   a. Key objectives
   b. Total costs and savings
   c. Labor requirements summary
   d. Principal problems
   e. Project priority criteria
2. Project identification
   a. Development and maintenance projects
   b. Labor requirements
      (1) Type of labor
      (2) Amount of labor
   c. Computer resource requirements for systems development, implementation, and operation
   d. Economic justification per project
      (1) Development cost
      (2) Implementation cost
      (3) Operation cost
      (4) Cash economies

        (5) Connections with other systems
        (6) Connections with other master plans
3. Hardware projections
    a. Existing applications
    b. New applications
    c. Survey of new hardware
    d. Hardware power organization strategy
    e. Hardware requirements
        (1) Mainframe
        (2) Storage
        (3) Space
        (4) Supplies
        (5) Other
4. Labor projections
    a. Labor needed in each job class
        (1) General nature
        (2) Development
        (3) Operation
    b. Salary levels, turnover estimates, training needs
5. Financial projections
    a. Hardware costs, depreciation, maintenance, space, air conditioning, electricity, etc.
    b. Labor, social benefits, training
    c. Miscellaneous: Building, telephone, outside service, etc.

6
Controlling the Cost of Data Services

This chapter discusses the main issues in the control of data services with particular emphasis on cost control of yearly operations. The first part deals with the general problem of control as postulated by accounting control theory, specifically in the context of data processing control. The second part discusses controls in the data processing acquisition/expansion phase. The next topic is controls in the operation of the information processing facility which are associated with the development of software, the preparation of data, the operation of the equipment, and the achievement of the objectives stated in the organization's data processing plan. Cost characteristics of data processing operations are then described. Costs are divided into fixed and variable, and the concept of equivalent annual cost is developed. Measures of performance are associated with the different elements of the data processing operation for evaluation purposes. The conclusion of the chapter integrates the concepts developed throughout the chapter into a unique control framework.

CONTROL

The strategic plan of an organization, as discussed in Chapter 1, is used as a framework to develop global system plans as well as particular plans for parts of the organization. These individual plans must incorporate

- Organizational objectives (e.g., maximize corporate profits over the long term)
- Organizational philosophies or strategies (e.g., vertical integration, lifetime employment)
- Department specific objectives (e.g., state-of-the-art computer technologies, data processing self-sufficiency)

- General policies (e.g., profit centers must break even; transfer prices must be at market rates)

Individual plans must also offer other more specific guidelines for the organization and its subentities. The loose terminology of *data processing facility* will be used to represent the aggregate of functions that have the primary responsibility for all computer-related activities for the organization. Matrix and distributed processing entities have problems and contexts of a somewhat different nature not specifically addressed herein. Organizational activities have past, present, and future elements (Vasarhelyi 1973) depicted in Figure 6.1.

The control activity is a comparison of actual economic activity with standards established in the planning process. This monitoring differentiates between standard and actual expenditures and forms noteworthy differences or variances that will lead to management action and/or a revision of standards.

A good example might be a data processing facility that has an annual budget of $120,000 for paper supplies. Assuming a constant rate of use, the budget should be $10,000 per month. If by the end of April $45,000 has already been spent, the difference of $5,000 needs to be accounted for. While it is reasonable to assume that some discrepancies will exist, the key question is which discrepancy requires further examination and management action? Rules of thumb prescribe that differences exceeding a certain percentage, say 10% of the cumulative budget, must be investigated. The above

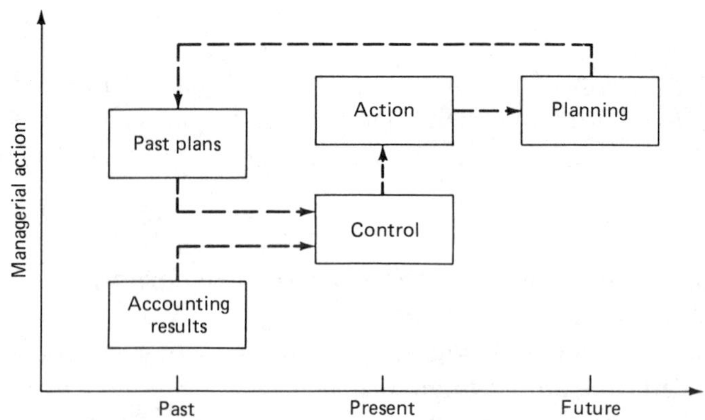

Figure 6.1. A normative view of the organization.

example shows a 12.5% discrepancy ([45,000 − 40,000]/40,000), which may require further investigation. This investigation may simply indicate that, for economic reasons, a certain minimum volume of preprinted forms must be ordered and that actual consumption was within a 2% variance. On the other hand, it may also reflect an increased consumption that must be reviewed or unrealistic budgeted levels will persist. Control, therefore, implies comparison of "actuals" and standards in the light of rules of acceptable variance.

Actual expenditures require timely reporting so that they may be compared against standards in time for remedial action. Standards may be formally or informally developed for this purpose. We will apply this theoretical framework to the control of the MIS department.

Figure 6.2 displays the organization chart of a typical data processing organization. The control objectives (EDPAA 1983) describe many of the functions to be kept in mind in relation to the boxes in the diagram.

STEERING COMMITTEE

The steering committee (executive committee) plays an essential role in the control and planning of the data processing facility. This committee is composed of a representative of top management and

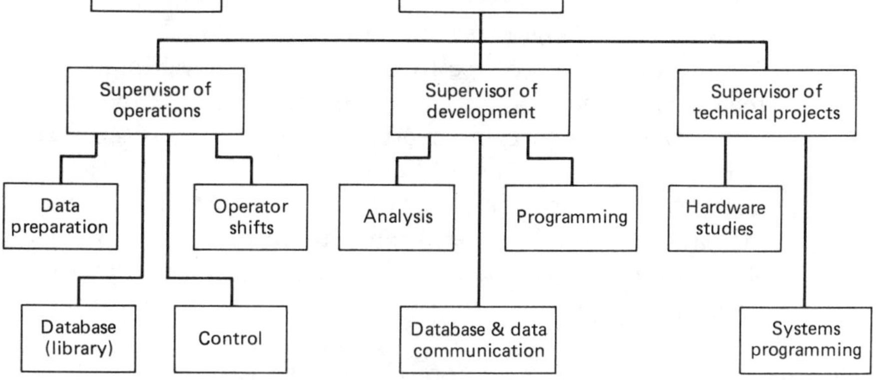

Figure 6.2. A typical MIS organization.

representatives from different groups within the company including key users, minority and/or potential users, and the MIS manager (with or without a vote). Its functions are managerial in nature: planning and control. The committee primarily serves in a planning capacity, setting the priorities of application projects and their respective schedules. Each project must have a proposed budget, natural project milestones, personnel and equipment plans, and operational objectives. Additionally, the committee will serve as a control for the achievement of objectives and fine tuning of the plan. It must be pointed out that only very large projects need to flow through the steering committee. The committee is strictly a planning and control device and should not interfere with executive issues such as equipment selection, personnel allocation, technical features of software, and very small projects.

The role of the MIS manager in relation to the steering committee is one of technical support and cost estimation. He is also an equal member of the committee. Users work with the MIS manager in estimating the cost and other requirements of proposed applications. The result of their effort comprises the zero base budgeting decision packages for the steering committee. For a more extensive discussion see Chapter 4.

Further examination of Figure 6.2 reveals two different types of processes to be controlled and managed:

1. The process controls related to computer operations are very similar to production line and job shop type of manufacturing. They require careful scheduling, management supervision, GANTT charts, and procedural training.
2. The second type of control relates to development and technical support activities which are similar to the control and management of engineering projects. It is often argued that these activities cannot be controlled. However, there are extensive writings about software maintenance and project management that are applicable to this problem. Utilizing the concept of zero base budgeting will provide a significant level of control.

Essential to this process is the development of projects with clear milestones and kill points. These should be spaced reasonably close to each other and, if at all possible, at logical project break points. Each stage should be defined at the best level of potential detail with clear breakdowns for: (1) costs, (2) labor to be used, (3) task to be completed, (4) hardware and software requirements necessary for the performance of the task, and (5) other project-specific details. All popular system development methodologies (SDM/70, Spectrum, etc.) specify these checkpoints.

In addition to a standard organizational chart, it is quite desirable to have a clear idea of standard expenditures within the data processing activity. Figure 6.3 shows several percentages of data processing budgets in relation to total sales in selected industries.

This figure displays substantial differences in data processing expenditures among industries but, if a very general rule-of-thumb is desired, one may assume that data processing budgets should be about 1% of gross sales. In addition, it is desirable to have an understanding of where money is being spent and what are the trends of these expenditures in order to control organizational data processing costs.

Figure 6.4 shows interesting patterns in data processing expenditures. In the last 10 years, hardware costs went from 39 to 31% of data processing budgets and it is projected that by the early 1990s, these costs will amount to 10% or less of the total MIS budget. On the other hand, the acquisition of software is growing not only in terms of the purchase of packaged software but also in terms of increased development costs. Figure 6.4 is somewhat misleading in the sense that about 20 to 30% of data processing expenditures are not part of the typical MIS budget. These expenditures, including the purchase of equipment such as word processors, communicators

	% Gross Sales
Supermarkets	0.2
Transportation	0.8
Electronic Equipment	1.2
Government	1.4
Insurance	1.6
Public Service	2.0
Universities	3.0

Figure 6.3. Data Processing costs by industry in relation to company sales, 1976.

	1972	*1978*	*1982*
Personnel	47%	51%	36%
Hardware	39	36	31
Software	1	2	10
Communications services	5	2	2
Media and supplies	6	7	11
Outside services	2	2	5
Miscellaneous	<1	<1	5

Source: Datamation, July 1982.

Figure 6.4. Standard composition of MIS budgets. Reprinted with permission of *Datamation*® magazine, © Copyright by Technical Publishing Company, A Dun & Bradstreet Company, 1982. All rights reserved.

and microprocessors as well as expenditures for communication lines, are often included in administrative or user budgets. As organizations evolve toward distributed data processing, we may find even further hidden data processing costs in user budgets.

Figures 6.3 and 6.4 will enable readers to compare their organizations with industry standards and to initiate an organizational cost breakdown diagnosis. The reader is warned against too much reliance upon simple formulas and rules-of-thumb.

In addition to general standards of cost, one must seriously consider the stage of development of one's own company's data processing function. A rather simplistic way of accomplishing this is by examining the age and technology of hardware being used. On the other hand, use of a modified version of Nolan's stages of EDP development growth (Nolan 1979) to classify stages of data processing evolution is preferred.

Stage I: INITIATION

The organization decides to acquire computing power whether through the acquisition of equipment or through some other modality of computer use. This initial effort involves top management approval but leads to very little top management involvement. Employees of the organization are redeployed and taught new skills. Behavioral resistance is found to be widespread in the areas of data processing exposure (Argyris 1971). Data processing costs are placed into organizational overhead with no assignment of a corporate charge to users.

Stage II: CONTAGION

The organization starts to use data processing in many areas of the company with several applications. The organizational environment favors the use of data processing as a symbol of competence and ability by those managers who adopt it. Top management becomes even less involved with data processing as its technical nature is frightening and unfamiliar. As accounting processes did not change, there is little consideration of cost/benefit tradeoffs in the adoption of data processing systems. This fact leads to capricious and status-oriented adoption of systems that do not pay for themselves either in economies of labor or in improvements of services and/or provision of information. Consequently, there is an explosion in data processing costs and utilization, leading to concerns by top management that will be reflected in the next stage.

Figure 6.5 displays a highly symbolic representation of the development of data processing stages. In it, the solid line delineates actual utilization of data processing, represented by some measure such as an MIS budget or number of applications, whereas the dotted line represents potential applications as demanded by the firm's market for data processing services. The gap between the two lines is the unsatisfied potential demand for computer services which will be only partially fulfilled by unilateral management efforts. The advent of "profit centers" and discretionary management leads to the ability

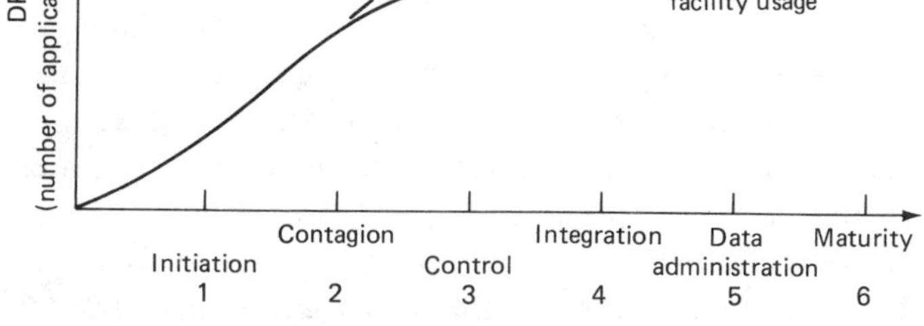

Figure 6.5. Stages of EDP growth. Reprinted by permission of the *Harvard Business Review*, "Managing the Crises in Data Processing," by Richard L. Nolan, March-April, 1979.

of managers to perform some data processing functions by themselves. For example, the cost of a microcomputer, even if fully configured, is probably less than $6,000. Managers can purchase such a system because this level of expenditure is substantially under their spending allowance. Furthermore, many of the modern engineering and production control machines are actually digital computers retrofitted for engineering use. These computers are progressively being supplied with higher-level languages such as BASIC and Pascal to satisfy demand. As an example, a division manager at a power utility may order a piece of equipment called a "load frequency control device" which is basically a small-sized computer with software and analog sensing devices to control the power generation and frequency in transmission lines. This basic hardware is a mainframe that, if properly supplied with software, can perform most of the functions of a business system. Therefore, the division manager, frustrated with the delays of a cost control system that he deems unnecessary, may utilize this type of equipment by hiring local college students on a part-time basis to develop software to meet his needs. This phenomenon of the proliferation of independent, unauthorized systems outside of the main budget and control mechanisms of organizational data processing is often called the "micro epidemics" and starts to occur late in the second stage and/or in the early part of the third stage of EDP growth.

Stage III: CONTROL

Management, concerned with the explosion of MIS-related costs and organizational bickering about priorities, decides to put a lid on MIS activities. At this stage there is often turnover of MIS management due to upper management's concern about an apparent lack of MIS control. Management techniques that were successful in stages I and II are no longer appropriate and, rather than try to change the habits of the MIS manager, upper management feels that because it is his fault that they are out of control, he should be replaced. One may also witness substantial changes in the style and philosophies of data processing development from this point on. The number of actual projects in process will decrease as substantial emphasis is given to system documentation, data quality, and accounting controls. The method of accounting for computer use may change from overhead to partial allocation which allows top management to allocate computer costs to operational units. Partial allocation enables management to stimulate the use of data processing in some units while limiting it in others.

Stage IV: INTEGRATION

The MIS department is joined with the end user departments so that corporate goals can be achieved more smoothly. MIS management starts to become more like businessmen and less technically oriented. This stage also calls for substantial top management involvement and for effective steering committees. Computer chargeout systems tend to be in a full allocation mode with few, if any, subsidized charges. Users have accepted the responsibility for their MIS-related charges and are learning how to control them.

Stage V: DATA ADMINISTRATION

This stage is a consequence of the fact that most organizations develop their MIS systems primarily as file systems (Nolan 1973). Included in this category are systems that, while they utilize data base management techniques, remain stand-alone, independent systems. These systems require integration into central data custody arrangements after a certain level of development. Substantial efforts are then devoted to system integration and the development of corporate data bases which once again serve to increase the gap between the demand and supply of computer systems.

Stage VI: MATURITY

This stage is represented by a global view of corporate resources and the philosophy that data is one of these resources. There tends to be sharing of data and associated costs by divisions as well as the intensive use of online data gathering, process control, and delegation of mechanical decision functions to the computer. At this stage, most organizations have decided their optimal mix of processing distribution and tend to support the minicomputers that spread throughout the organization in prior stages.

A general caveat must be placed against the use of the Stage Theory of EDP development. Nolan specifies that four characteristics of an organization determine its stage: the application portfolio, data processing technology and staff experience, user awareness, and management controls. Organizations, however, evolve heterogeneously and, while certain areas might be at a mature data processing stage, one may find other areas rather immature. In addition, the technological stage of corporate hardware is not necessarily a good indicator of data processing maturity.

The acquisition and expansion stages of hardware pose a substantially different cost control problem than the cost control of EDP operations. The next section will address these issues.

CONTROLS FOR THE INITIATION STAGE

Acquisition of computer software and hardware requires careful analysis of corporate options. As an organization considers acquiring computer power, it must explore the desirability of such an endeavor as opposed to continuing with manual processes. The key problem in this initial exploration stage is that the organization usually does not have anyone with competence in data processing to perform this task.

Three potential paths may be used in acquiring computer power:

1. Establishment of an MIS department whose purpose includes the acquisition of computer hardware, operating personnel, and systems development personnel.
2. Utilization of a service bureau or other external data center.
3. The contracting for full computer services provided by a separate company.

The first and second alternatives require substantial learning by the user organization that is the main party in the management and use of the computer. The third option involves the hiring of an organization to provide full computer services while the user firm concentrates on the preparation and use of the data. In recent years many organizations have been created to provide this type of service – Automated Data Processing, for example. Additionally, with the advent of minicomputers and microcomputers, organizations can buy fully dedicated "turnkey" systems delivered with hardware and software ready for use, requiring only operation and data preparation by the user.

The key considerations for this first-stage decision are mainly related to organizational aims and corporate skills. The firm must be able to respond to a series of sensitive questions such as:

1. Should we devote a substantial part of our managerial talent to the management of data processing (DP)?
2. Would data processing operations substantially free management time from other functions to compensate for the time invested in DP affairs?
3. Do we have to utilize computer technologies for the long-term survival of the firm?
4. Are we becoming technologically obsolete without data processing? Is the competition doing it?

Let us illustrate these issues with a real-life example. A small property management firm based in New York was looking for a computer system to administer about 40 properties with about 600 living units. The firm, AFA, had two principals that were the brains of the business. One of the principals was dedicated to sales and marketing while the other concentrated on the day-to-day management of the properties.

The operations partner took a computer introduction class in night school and was convinced that the firm needed a small computer. He examined three typical options:

1. The purchase of a small turnkey system for about $80,000.
2. The purchase of a small IBM System 32 for $40,000 and the contracting of an experienced software development house for about $30,000 to develop the system in six months.
3. The utilization of a service bureau for about $600 per month.

On the advice of an outside consultant they decided to take the third option for three reasons:

1. Because their business was property management, they could not afford further distractions for the operations manager.

2. Cash requirements for purchase were too steep for them at that point in time.
3. Utilizing the service bureau would teach them enough to eventually purchase a system.

The epilogue of the story is a sad one. The partners had a major fight over personal expenses and the operations partner left to work for an oil supply company. In the ensuing confusion, several customers took their buildings to other property management firms. Although its client list was substantially reduced, AFA managed to survive because of the small amount of fixed costs. It is most likely that the firm would have declared bankruptcy if it had an $80,000 computer loan obligation.

The initial set of feasibility questions should be followed by a more serious analysis of hardware/software selection. As the story illustrates, when selection and feasibility questions overlap, some key considerations on hardware/software acquisition should be outlined.

1. *Cost:* The equivalent purchase cost of the particular item. Cost comparision should be performed using the minimum equivalent purchase cost derived from outright declared purchase cost or the present value of the stream of lease payments necessary to keep the equipment for its expected service life (say, seven years). Monthly maintenance costs should also be considered. The discount rate used should be the incremental borrowing cost for the firm.

   For example, consider the purchase of an IBM System 34 with 128K of memory, 64Mb of disk storage, a 650 lines-per-minute printer, four terminals, and a floppy disk unit. Assume a purchase price of $70,000 or a monthly lease charge of $3,030. In addition, both alternatives require monthly hardware and operating software maintenance charges of $250.

   In our analysis we will assume a four year decision horizon that will simply extend the lease of the computer for a year after the initial three year term, and the salvage value of the computer will be negligible. Figure 6.6 displays a comparative table.

OPTION	MONTHLY COST OF BORROWING	PRINCIPAL	ANNUITY	TOTAL
Purchase	1.0%	70,000	19,930	89,630
Lease	1.0%		115,491	115,491
Purchase	1.5%	70,000	17,598	87,598
Lease	1.5%		103,141	103,141
Purchase	2.0%	70,000	15,856	85,856
Lease	2.0%		92,930	92,930
Purchase	2.5%	70,000	14,357	84,357
Lease	2.5%		84,143	84,143
Purchase	3.0%	70,000	13,059	83,059
Lease	3.0%		76,538	76,538

Figure 6.6. Equivalent purchase costs, IBM System 34.

This figure shows that under an incremental monthly borrowing cost of 1, 1.5, or 2%, the purchase option is more interesting. At a 2.5% borrowing cost the options are equivalent and at a 3% discount rate the lease would be preferable. This analysis ignores the effects of taxes where depreciation and interest costs may play an important part. Even though, it is hoped, interest rates may have declined by the time you read this book, a similar analysis can be performed at any level.

It should also be noted that rental costs of the vendor-supplied software were identical in both alternatives and were ignored in this analysis. On the other hand, in the evaluation of the project as a whole, these costs must be included. For illustration purposes, we shall assume that the internal (or external) costs of funds for the organization is 1% per month leading to the present purchase value of \$89,630 or \$99,122 including the present value of an annuity of 48 payments of \$250 for maintenance (vendor increases not withstanding).

2. *Supplier reliability:* It is important to be able to estimate the likelihood of a failure or a change in attitude on the part of the supplier. Major U.S. corporations have already ventured into the computer market and withdrawn at substantial losses for themselves and their clients. Financial figures, corporate

reputation, and the industry "grapevine" may serve to give guidance in this matter.

3. *Quality of maintenance:* The terms of the maintenance contract, the experience of other users, and a maintenance history from the supplier will serve to evaluate this variable.
4. *Obsolescence:* There are advantages and disadvantages for state-of-the-art equipment that should be carefully weighed. A corporation may wisely opt for the used computer market in order to decrease acquisition costs and software instability. However, the pros and cons of dephasing with current technology must be weighed.
5. *Terms of supply:* Equipment availability and delivery schedules as well as system installation support are variables in the hardware selection process. These must be carefully evaluated in order to assess how realistic are the vendor's promised delivery schedules. Surprisingly, different suppliers (dealers) may be able to provide substantially different delivery schedules based on the sale price of a piece of equipment.
6. *Availability of software:* This variable, which was of lesser importance in earlier years, has become one of the most important factors in the current state of turnkey systems and packaged software.

EDP CENTER OPERATION CONTROLS

Figure 6.4 describes the standard breakdown of costs of a data center as related to general MIS budget allocations. Organizationally, budgets are broken down by division and not by particular MIS function. Therefore, items like personnel, supplies, and hardware are often found in different divisions.

The cost control problem in a data center facility, as in many other functional areas, can be analyzed to provide information for:

- Operations controls
- Management and strategic planning processes

Although we stressed the use of equivalent purchase costs in acquisition analysis, a different method may be desirable for the second item above. Firms that acquire computer equipment and do not allocate its cost over the equipment's life span will have substantially understated MIS costs over the long term.

In addition, one must understand the inherent nature of the different types of computer costs. The total computer cost curve is clearly a semivariable one with a fixed component and variable component. On the other hand, the increase of one unit of computer output (processing) is quite negligible in comparison to the large amount of resources necessary to produce an additional system.

In data processing, therefore, incremental production costs should be differentiated in its three main areas:

1. Applications development, a very labor-intensive activity, requires additional personnel for each project. It is possible to budget and staff a data processing center in a way that all production and maintenance can be done, with no additional resources required unless additional software is desired.
2. The same is not completely true for technical support because a minimum staff of system programmers and administrative staff must be maintained. Therefore, there is less flexibility for cost control in this area.
3. In the operations area, incremental costs are very small and restricted to supplies, energy, and recording media, unless there are substantial hardware increases.

Figure 6.7 consists of three different cost curves representing a hypothetical situation. The horizontal axis represents the amount of work processed and the vertical axis represents the cost of operation.

Clearly, costs that are fixed are easier to manage but cannot be reduced when necessary. Variable costs that make up the larger portion of the MIS cost structure can be manipulated as the need arises. Consequently, during bad economic times, development of new systems grinds to a halt for quick cost savings. Of course, this economizing occurs precisely when the investment in efficiency of operations should be made.

Martin Buss, a consultant with Arthur D. Little, Inc., states that "controlling data processing by controlling costs can have unexpected consequences, as a number of companies have found out. These companies have discovered that they have devoted insufficient

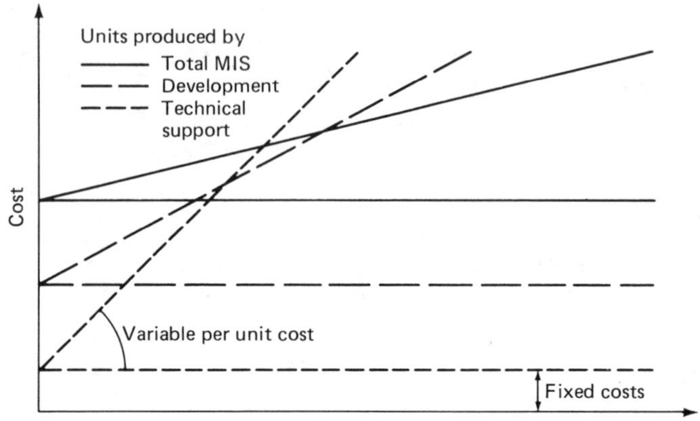

Figure 6.7. Cost structures. Reprinted by permission of the *Harvard Business Review,* "Penny-Wise Approach to Data Processing," by M.D. Buss, July-August 1981.

resources to data processing, and as a result they are not faced with large investments in new programming."

He argues for a controlled expansion of data processing costs within the boundaries of inflation and industry DP costs. Figure 6.8 displays his figures.

A chart such as Figure 6.8 can be developed for most industries in which data processing expenditures may be gauged. Some organizations have managed to obtain substantial competitive advantages by investing heavily in data processing. Among these are American Airlines (SABRE) and Avis (Wizard of Avis). The first managed to directly capitalize on their technological advantage by selling direct terminal connections to independent travel agents and imposing a penalty on reservations for travel on other airlines made through

	Inflation CPI		All Industry DP costs	
Year	%	Indexed	% Change	Indexed
1975	9.1	109	13	113
1976	5.8	115	12	127
1977	6.5	123	10	139
1978	7.6	132	12	158
1979	11.5	147	12	175
5 year growth rate	8%		11.8%	

Figure 6.8. Percentage changes for cost comparisons.

their system. This marketing advantage led to a fierce battle for the connection to the travel agent market where United Airlines and others are now trying to compete with American.

These caveats indicate the need for careful reflection before instituting cost-cutting measures in data processing centers. The variable versus fixed cost considerations show that often the most important functions go first in a tight economy while vested interest and lack of foresight leave a great deal of fat in operations as fixed costs.

In addition to cost budgets, time budgets are often used as a way to control development activities. On the other hand, production schedules serve as time controls for production efforts. The setting of time objectives is essential in system planning and in the process of OS/360 by IBM or the previously mentioned SABRE system exceeded time and cost budgets by 100%. These early and valiant efforts, though justifiable within their context and period, are not acceptable in light of modern computer technologies and experience. Managers are often told that estimating time and cost in software projects is not feasible. This is absolutely not true anymore except in certain very highly technical or innovative projects. Project managers should be expected to come within 10% of their time and cost budgets but may be allowed to renegotiate them at natural check points.
may be allowed to renegotiate them at natural check points.

Of course, the most important form of data center control is close and competent supervision by well-trained managers. No scheme of management or budgeting will serve better as a control than a highly motivated, knowledgeable manager. Managers must be motivated to bring projects in on time and at budget with a clear schedule of rewards and penalties. Underbidders or overbidders should be aware that such behavior is not condoned since it is highly detrimental to the application selection process as a whole.

Examinations by internal or external auditors also serve as a control mechanism but have little bearing on the day-to-day operations of data processing. Standards of control can be found in publications by the EDP Auditors Association (e.g., EDPAA, *Control Objectives,* 1983) or other entities such as the Canadian Institute or the Institute of Internal Auditors.

The cost characteristics of the data processing activity must be carefully integrated with the scheme of computer charges and the nature of the organization.

COSTING SCHEMES AND COST CHARACTERISTICS

This chapter describes three types of charging schemes: (1) overhead charges, (2) partial chargeout, and (3) chargeout schemes. These schemes only demonstrate how to allocate charges among competing entities such as a "responsibility center." The other problem that must be considered is how much to charge for a particular unit of computer services. Two general methods exist: (1) market prices and (2) cost schemes.

The first approach basically estimates the cost of acquiring similar services from an outside supplier and allows cost allocations on this basis. This type of approach, where a market mechanism may be in action, is often used in highly decentralized profit-center oriented organizations. It motivates managers to run a cost-efficient data processing shop because the MIS managers are evaluated in terms of the profit they make. It also may allow for a substantial exodus of business that may be processed in-house from the firm.

The second, a cost approach or a cost-plus approach, basically estimates the data processing budget and the data processing use, and makes a unit charge for the different types of services. Though less emotionally costly and productive of fewer interdivisional disputes about processing changes it does not actively promote data processing effectiveness. It may, however, prevent some short-term, nonproductive behavior.

Olson and Ives (1982) studied chargeout systems with particular emphasis on what they called the "user interface" of the chargeout system. They used Nolan's (1977) characteristics of these interfaces, which were: (1) understandability, (2) controllability, (3) accountability, and (4) cost benefit incidence. After examining 23 organizations and separating their chargeout schemes for operations and development, they found mixed results that do not necessarily favor any of the alternative chargeout schemes.

Ordinarily, operations are measured on the basis of a series of variables such as:

- CPU use
- Storage medium use
- I/O requests
- Level of operator intervention

These variables are aggregated into a formula containing unit rates for each variable. For example, the CPU is measured in seconds and multiplied by a rate of, say, $270 per hour, to arrive at a partial job charge. In similar fashion, tape mounts could be charged at $2.00 each. These rates are adjusted until a desired revenue level is attained.

In order to encourage end users to use a different hardware mix, the individual rate can be adjusted. In other words, if one wishes to encourage the use of a laser printer instead of a line printer, they would set the rate per page at 5 cents for the laser printer and 10 cents for the line printer.

Systems development and maintenance are charged out based on:

1. DP personnel time allocated
2. Overhead of management costs
3. Direct development costs in terms of machine use of debugging runs within the operations algorithms

Figure 6.9 illustrates the cost schemes as charged to users at a major U.S. university operating DEC 20/60 and IBM 4341 model 2 computers.

The development of a comprehensive and satisfactory cost allocation scheme is a very difficult and time-consuming task. It requires competent DP management and maturity from the users within the organization. As we discussed earlier, the nature of the cost allocation method changes over the stages of maturation of the data processing effort. Specific chargeout methodologies are discussed in greater detail in Chapter 8.

SUGGESTIONS FOR COST CONTROLS

Despite the possibility of draconian measures of project cuts and freezes in data processing activities, the most promising route for a data processing activity that is effective (doing the right thing) and efficient (doing the thing right) is through careful control and examination within a planning framework of all data processing activities.

The systems development life cycle is a very useful tool for this control. Its key features were suggested by Shaw and Atkins (1970). A modified version of such a system development process is described in Figure 6.10.

```
DEC-20 Usage Report for Project Number 0022873
Billing Period: 1-Jun-82 to 30-Jun-82                 Statement Generated 8-Jul-82
***********************************************************************************

                        ***SUMMARY OF TOTALS***

GSB1 Totals:
  112 page-days disk storage                                        $     0.56
  Total charges...................................................$      0.56

Grand Totals for Project Number 0022873
  122 online sessions, used 534:42.537 in 143:17:10                 $ 1072.14
  2 batch sessions, used 06,692 in 0:02:01                          $     0.15
  119 output requests, 2684 units in 70 files                       $    47.86
  23194 page-days, disk storage                                     $   160.97
  1 structure mounts, connected 0:00:38                             $     2.26
  0 tapes                                                           $     0.000
  0 disk packs                                                      $     0.000
  Miscellaneous changes                                             $     0.00
  Miscellaneous credits                                             $     0.00
  Allocation of funds                                               $10000.00
  Deallocation of funds                                             $     0.00
  Minimum charge adjustments                                        $     0.00

Total balance adjustment = $—8716;  total charge (not counting allocations) = $1283.38

                         ******************
                         * TOTAL CHARGE   *
                         * $      1283.38 *
                         ******************


                          IBM 4341 Mod 2
                 TOTALS FOR ACCOUNT: 0068849
                    FOR PERIOD STARTING 06/01/82 AT 10:32:05
                    AND ENDING 07/01/82 AT 10:28:11
                  CMSBATCH JOBS:                        $3.41
                  CMSBATCH DED. DEVICES:                $0.00
                  CMSBATCH TDISK:                       $0.00
                  VM INTERACTIVE USE:               $2,986.04
                  VM INTER. DED. DEVICES:             $246.54
                  VM INTERACTIVE TDISK:                 $7.34
                  PERMANENT MINI-DISKS:               $310.00
                  REAL PRINT, PUNCH OUTPUT:         $1,138.08
                  OS/VSI WYLBUR SESSIONS:               $0.00
                  OS/VSI JOBS:                          $0.00
                  GOULD USE:                            $0.00
                  CREDITS:                              $0.00
                  DEBITS:                               $0.00
                                                 **************
                  TOTAL COST:                    *  $4,691.41 *
                                                 **************
```

Figure 6.9. Sample computer charges.

As a very general rule, about 40% of a systems development effort goes into systems planning and analysis, 30% into programming, and 30% into systems testing and implementation.

The trade-offs of effort are quite clear: if a firm increases its expenditures in the first stage, the risk associated with the projects

PLANNING AND ANALYSIS

- Existing System Survey and Initial Investigation
- Preliminary System Design
- Management Approval Steering Committee Approval

DEVELOPMENT ACTIVITIES

- Analysis and Detailed Systems Design
- User Approval
- Programming
- User Training
- Systems Testing and User Acceptance Testing
- User Approval

IMPLEMENTATION ACTIVITIES

- Conversion of Data
- Parallel Operation
- Implementation
- Post Implementation Review
- Ongoing Maintenance

Figure 6.10. System life cycle.

decreases. On the other hand, the amount of committed resources that may eventually have to be abandoned is larger.

Existing System Survey and Initial Investigation

The initial systems investigation basically provides a statement of the problem to be considered and the desired outcome. It is usually related to a survey of existing systems to make sure that the desired functions are not already being performed. This step must be performed since we often find repetitive functions in large corporate MIS departments.

Preliminary System Study

This step takes an in-depth view of the system by specifying reports, input data, and processing to be accomplished. In addition, data flows, processes, and internal controls are prescribed with particular care for the transaction audit trail. The conclusion of this process leads to the preparation of a detailed systems proposal and/or a decision package for the zero base budgeting system. This is a natural kill point for a data processing project.

Analysis and System Requirements

This step involves the detailed analysis of the system to be developed, the design of forms, and the specification of system interfaces. At the completion of this phase, complete documentation of the system has been prepared except for actual program coding.

Programming and User Training

This phase includes the actual coding of the system and should be performed in parallel with the initial stages of user training and orientation. At this stage, careful attention should be paid to the usage of reusable code and the construction of an efficient data dictionary. Some organizations forbid communication between programmers and analysts in an effort to improve the documentation that will serve as the main communication medium for system maintenance. This philosophy should not be condoned in an industry where good communication is difficult at best.

SUMMARY AND CONCLUSIONS

This chapter presented an integrated view of data processing control issues. It initially developed a theory of control and integrated it with the organizational planning process. It developed a typical MIS organization chart and divided MIS activities into processing, development, and technical support. The role of the steering committee was carefully defined as a planning and control body composed of active users and top management acting as a powerful advisor to MIS management and as a representative of the political wishes of the corporate entity.

The chapter concentrated on defining the differences between production and development control, giving guidelines for average industry expenses. The stages of EDP growth were defined as initiation, contagion, control, integration, data administration, and maturity. Furthermore, the key issues in acquiring computer power and the selection of equipment were illustrated. Considerations included cost, supplier reliability, quality of maintenance, obsolescence, terms of supply, and availability of software.

Cost allocation schemes and the nature of data processing costs strongly influence how organizations proceed in data processing and under what limitations they must operate. Data processing maturity seems to indicate further and more widespread cost chargeouts.

7
Automation and Modeling

The single most prevalent reason for the failure of zero base budgeting in a company is the level of effort needed to generate and process the tremendous amounts of required data. In this context, failure means that zero base budgeting is utilized once and then abandoned because of the sheer cost of its development and use. Failure does not preclude participants from receiving a great deal of value from the process, however. At a minimum, they identify even the smallest activity unknown to all except the person working on it. They also identify activities that benefit no one.

In an examination of the ZBB process, it should be intuitively obvious which steps can be automated to relegate the data handling to a machine suited to the task. The systems flow for a typical ZBB process is pictured in Figure 7.1. Note the iterations involved in refining the data contents and the multitude of reports required. Considering that the computer still has a great deal of trouble gathering information from people's brains or other nondigitized sources, we will assume that the activity information is keyed by a clerk or even the manager responsible for creating the data. Humans are also reluctant to delegate the analysis and decision making to the computer but surely MIS can help. Computers are clearly being used more and more to capture, manipulate, and report activity information.

It has been demonstrated that the clerical and statistical efforts in using ZBB can be reduced by 50 to 75% with even the implementation of the most basic computer system. The activity packages themselves are revised at least once during the review process and, rather than type them two or more times, it is obviously better to key them into an automated system. Then one must only be concerned with changing a single line and reprinting a given package. The use of computerized models enables the manager to use "what if" techniques to manipulate the data and experiment with different alternatives. Certain priorities can be raised or lowered and the results presented

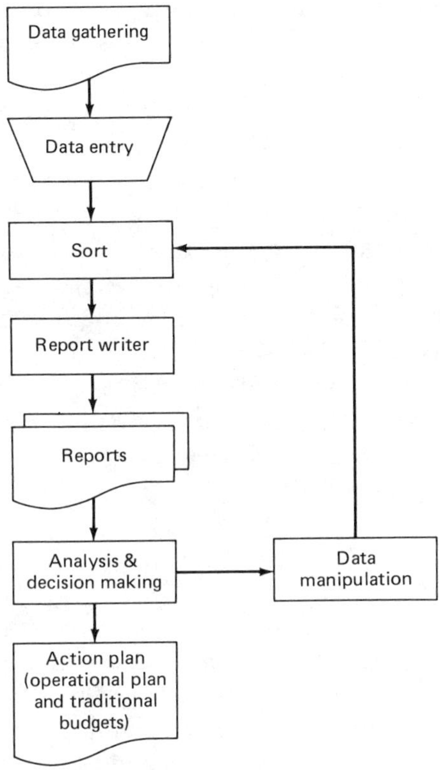

Figure 7.1. Systems flow chart.

to the end user for consideration. The cost of resources can be manipulated to reflect contemplated increases or a certain staff level could be added. For example, if a new type of staff position is to fit in between the current 34 and 35 grade levels, an analysis of new expenditure levels is readily available.

If the total MIS function is widely distributed around the country and all parts are included in the ZBB process, centralize the data base or use electronic mail techniques to eliminate mail delays. Updating the packages because of the addition of new assumptions and disseminating that information will take only a few minutes instead of days.

The cost of computerization is minute compared to the savings in management time. The entire system can be programmed in a high-level language in a matter of days, a week at most. Assuming that it takes a programmer/analyst a week to design, code, and test the system and also that the salary rate is $20.00 per hour, only about 25 hours of management time needs to be saved in order to break even. This does not even consider the adverse affects of taking them away from their real management functions for clerical tasks.

Once you have decided that ZBB should be applied to your department and after you have tailored the ideas presented in this book, develop the software to aid in the process before the first byte of data is gathered. Provide the ability to easily input the original data, modify that data, and report it back in a variety of ways. You will need to use a responsive report writer and not a typical programming language such as COBOL. Despite the preponderance of variable word combinations and unstructured sentences, the ZBB application is not suited for your word processor. Perhaps as the WP/DP interface develops, we may have to retract this statement but for now, let us categorize ZBB as a data processing application.

CHOICE OF TOOLS IMPORTANT

The nature of this application is one that requires easy data input, a variety of reporting possibilities, and very little processing logic. The use of graphics is recommended as a communication tool for management presentations of your recommendations. This application could easily be put on a microcomputer and programmed in a variety of languages. Using BASIC, however, does not provide a responsive enough reporting tool. For purposes of demonstration, we have utilized a high-level reporting language on an IBM mainframe. The specific tool is not as critical as the methodology used.

FOCUS is primarily an online data base query language that was designed specifically for the nontechnical end user but can be used by the data processor for simple systems and prototyping larger systems. It is easy to learn and is available from Information Builders Inc., 1250 Broadway, New York, NY 10001. The FIDEL module, which is a FOCUS Input Data Entry Language, was used to input the original data and also for correction of data. All FOCUS code and reports are presented in this chapter.

Other high-level languages can also be utilized. A few that come to mind are SAS, MARK IV, Easytrieve, and even TSO/SPF in conjunction with a report writer.

DATA BASE DESIGN

Utilizing these high-level languages, we really do not have to design a data base in the strictest sense but merely have to identify each data element and its characteristics. Figure 7.2 represents such a data base description, and Figure 7.3 is the coded FOCUS file narrative. As a good systems analyst can tell you, this is the most critical part of the entire automation process. If the data element is not identified in the beginning, it is a chore to add it later. This design should be completed before your activity package is designed and before any reports are coded.

PROCESSING LOGIC

As stated above, there is very little processing that needs to be done. Editing criteria is basically limited to numeric tests and

Item	*Length*	*Alpha/numeric*
Activity number		
Prime number	3	Num
Activity level	1	Num
Activity name	15	A/N
Department (data processing)	2	Num
Sponsor (user)	2	Num
Staff grade level (5 occurrences)	2 ea	Num
Mandays (for each grade level)	4 ea	Num
Priority	1	Num
Current level	1	A/N
Activity description	100	A/N
Activity scope	100	A/N
Objectives	100	A/N
Advantages	100	A/N
Disadvantages	100	A/N
Alternatives	100	A/N
Consequences	100	A/N
Savings	6	Num
Start date	6	Num
End date	6	Num
Dependencies (upon other activ.)	4 ea	Num
Project/continuing activity	1	A/N

Figure 7.2. Activity data base.

```
FILENAME=ACTIVITY,SUFFIX=FOC
SEGNAME=ACTDESC,SEGTYPE=S1
FIELD=ACTIV NUMB,ALIAS=ACTNO,FORMAT=I4,$
FIELD=ACTIV NAME,ALIAS=ACTNA,FORMAT=A15,$
FIELD=SPONSOR,ALIAS=SPON,FORMAT=A2,$
FIELD=PRIORITY,ALIAS=PRTY,FORMAT=A1,$
FIELD=CURR LEVEL,ALIAS=CURR,FORMAT=A1,$
FIELD=SAVINGS,ALIAS=SAVES,FORMAT=I6C,$
FIELD=START DATE,ALIAS=START,FORMAT=16MDY,$
FIELD=ENDDATE,ALIAS=ENDDATE,FORMAT=16MDY,$
FIELD=CONTIN/PROJ,ALIAS=CONT,FORMAT=A1,$
FIELD=ACTIV DESC,ALIAS=DESC,FORMAT=A100,$
FIELD=ACTIV SCOPE,ALIAS=SCOPE,FORMAT=A100,$
FIELD=ADVANTAGES,ALIAS=ADVAN,FORMAT=A100,$
FIELD=DISADVANTAGE,ALIAS=DISADV,FORMAT=A100,$
FIELD=ALTERNATIVES,ALIAS=ALT,FORMAT=A100,$
FIELD=CONSEQUENCES,ALIAS=CONS,FORMAT=A100,$
FIELD=OBJECTIVES,ALIAS=OBJ,FORMAT=A100,$
FIELD=DEPENDENCIES,ALIAS=DEPEND,FORMAT=A12,$
SEGNAME=DEPART,SEGTYPE=S1,PARENT=ACTDESC
FIELD=DEPARTMENT,ALIAS=DEPT,FORMAT=A2,$
SEGNAME=STAFF,SEGTYPE=S1,PARENT=DEPART
FIELD=GRADE,,FORMAT=A2,$
FIELD=MANDAYS,,FORMAT=I4C,$
```

Figure 7.3.

validation of codes. The following is a list of potential edit criteria for the data base described in Figure 7.2:

Item	*Edit Criteria*
Department	Match to code list
Sponsor	Match to code list
Grade Level	Match to code list
Mandays	Numeric
Priority	1 through 6
Current Level	At, Above or Below
Savings	Numeric
Dates	Month from 1 to 12
	Day from 1 to 31
	Year over 1982
Proj/contin	Match to code list

A few items should be encoded before entry into the system and decoded for reporting purposes. These include: Department, Sponsor, Grade Level, Approval Status, Current Level, and Project/Continuing Activity.

There are also two data values that should be kept in a program table:

Full-time Equivalent Factor (FTE): used to convert manday estimates to number of people. If one takes vacations, holidays, sick time, and more into account, an average of 17 man-days per month or 200 per year is acceptable.

Cost per FTE: needs to be determined for each grade level. A level 35 senior systems analyst, for example, might earn $40,000 per year and receive additional employee benefits of 30% for insurance, employer FICA, bonus, and so forth. The annual cost factor for this grade would be $52,000.

REPORTING

It is critical to the information-modeling process to prepare various reports in order to view the data base from different vantage points. Reiterating suggestions made earlier: do not use COBOL; use a high-level report writer. Outlined below are reporting possibilities and the purpose of each. Where appropriate, the report has been programmed and included in the examples.

1. Headcount Reconciliation

Figure: 7.4.

Content: Activities at or below current levels.

Sequence: Department, Grade Level, Activity Number.

Totals: Grade Level, Department, Grand

```
HEADCOUNT RECONCILIATION - AT & BELOW CURRENT LEVELS

              DEPARTMENT: PROGRAMMING

                                  FULL TIME
GRADE  NUMBER  ACTIVITY NAME      EQUIVALENT      COST
-----  ------  -------------      ----------      ----
35     134-5   BILLING SYSTEM           1.15    57,500
       141-1   MAINTAIN G/L              .50    25,000
       142-1   MAINTAIN A/P              .25    12,500

*TOTAL GRADE 35
                                        1.90    95,000

34     105-1   MAINTAIN P/R             1.00    45,000

*TOTAL GRADE 34
                                        1.00    45,000
*TOTAL DEPARTMENT 01
                                        2.90   140,000
```

Figure 7.4.

HEADCOUNT RECONCILIATION - AT & BELOW CURRENT LEVELS

DEPARTMENT: TECH SERVICES

GRADE	NUMBER	ACTIVITY NAME	FULL TIME EQUIVALENT	COST
35	201-1	MAINTAIN SCP	2.00	100,000
	201-2	INSTALL VM	2.00	100,000
	202-2	LOCAL VTAM	.50	25,000
	202-3	REMOTE VTAM	.38	18,750
*TOTAL GRADE 35			4.88	243,750
34	143-1	MAINTAIN DYL250	.20	9,000
	202-1	MAINTAIN BTAM	.50	22,500
*TOTAL GRADE 34			.70	31,500
*TOTAL DEPARTMENT 02			5.57	275,250
TOTAL			8.47	415,250

Figure 7.4 cont'd.

Purpose: Used to balance current activities to current headcount. Will identify time not accounted for which will result in the identification of additional activities or adjustment of the manpower-required estimate. Consideration should be given to those activities requiring one grade level but which are currently being performed by another. In this situation, the individual grade levels will not balance to existing staff levels but the department totals will balance, all other things being equal.

2. Activity Control List

Figure: 7.5.

Content: Basic descriptive information.

Sequence: Activity Number, Department, Grade Level.

Totals: Grand.

Purpose: Primarily a printout of the key elements of the data base for quick reference. Helpful when trying to resolve inconsistencies or coordinating effort levels of multiple departments.

3. Activities by Sponsor

Figure: 7.6.

Content: Key information for each sponsor including: Activity Number, Cost, FTE, and Priority.

ACTIVITY CONTROL LIST

NUMBR	DEPTNAME	GRADE	ACTIVITY NAME	AT ABOVE OR BELOW CURRENT	FTE	COST	PRIORITY	SPONNAME	DEPENDENCIES
105-1	PROGRAMMING	34	MAINTAIN P/R	AT	1.00	45,000	6	ACCOUNTING	NONE
134-5	PROGRAMMING	35	BILLING SYSTEM	ABOVE	1.15	57,500	6	ACCOUNTING	1344
141-1	PROGRAMMING	35	MAINTAIN G/L	AT	.50	25,000	5	ACCOUNTING	0000
142-1	PROGRAMMING	35	MAINTAIN A/P	AT	.25	12,500	5	ACCOUNTING	0000
143-1	TECH SERVICES	34	MAINTAIN DYL250	BELOW	.20	9,000	2	PROGRAMMING	NONE
201-1	TECH SERVICES	35	MAINTAIN SCP	AT	2.00	100,000	6	TECH SERVICES	NONE
201-2	TECH SERVICES	35	INSTALL VM	ABOVE	2.00	100,000	3	TECH SERVICES	NONE
202-1	TECH SERVICES	34	MAINTAIN BTAM	AT	.50	22,500	6	TECH SERVICES	NONE
202-2	TECH SERVICES	35	LOCAL VTAM	ABOVE	.50	25,000	3	TECH SERVICES	NONE
202-3	TECH SERVICES	35	REMOTE VTAM	AT	.38	18,750	3	TECH SERVICES	NONE

Figure 7.5.

ACTIVITIES BY SPONSOR
DEPARTMENT - ACCOUNTING

PRIORITY	NUMBR	ACTIVITY NAME	AT ABOVE OR BELOW CURRENT	FULL TIME EQUIVALENT	COST	DEPTNAME
6	105-1	MAINTAIN P/R	AT	1.00	45,000	PGMG
	134-5	BILLING SYSTEM	ABOVE	1.15	57,500	PGMG
*TOTAL PRIORITY 6				2.15	102,500	
5	141-1	MAINTAIN G/L	AT	.50	25,000	PGMG
	142-1	MAINTAIN A/P	AT	.25	12,500	PGMG
*TOTAL PRIORITY 5				.75	37,500	
*TOTAL SPONSOR 01				2.90	140,000	
2	143-1	MAINTAIN DYL250	BELOW	.20	9,000	TECH
*TOTAL PRIORITY 2				.20	9,000	
*TOTAL SPONSOR 91				.20	9,000	
6	201-1	MAINTAIN SCP	AT	2.00	100,000	TECH
	202-1	MAINTAIN BTAM	AT	.50	22,500	TECH
*TOTAL PRIORITY 6				2.50	122,500	
3	201-2	INSTALL VM	ABOVE	2.00	100,000	TECH
	202-2	LOCAL VTAM	ABOVE	.50	25,000	TECH
	202-3	REMOTE VTAM	AT	.38	18,750	TECH
*TOTAL PRIORITY 3				2.88	143,750	
*TOTAL SPONSOR 92				5.38	266,250	
TOTAL				8.47	415,250	

Figure 7.6.

Sequence: Sponsor, Priority, Activity, Department, Grade Level.

Totals: Priority, Sponsor, Grade.

Purpose: Itemize activities that will be or are sponsored by each end user department. That is, activities with priorities 4, 5, and 6 need to be funded, and, presumably, the sponsor provides the funds in his budget.

4. Activities by Department

Figure: 7.7.

Content: Key information for each manager including: Activity Number, Cost, FTE, and Priority.

Sequence: Department, Priority, Sponsor, Grade Level.

Totals: Priority, Department, Grand.

Purpose: Itemizes activities that are or will be performed by each data processing department and is the basis for its budget. That is, activities with priorities 4, 5, and 6 will be performed during the year, and the staff must be provided for.

ACTIVITIES BY DEPARTMENT
DEPARTMENT - PGMG

PRIORITY	SPONSOR	GRADE	NUMBR	ACTIVITY NAME	AT ABOVE OR BELOW CURRENT	FTE	COST	PRIORITY	CURRDESC
6	01	34	105-1	MAINTAIN P/R	AT	1.00	45,000	6	AT
		35	134-5	BILLING SYSTEM	ABOVE	1.15	57,500	6	ABOVE
*TOTAL PRIORITY 6						2.15	102,500		
5	01	35	141-1	MAINTAIN G/L	AT	.50	25,000	5	AT
		35	142-1	MAINTAIN A/P	AT	.25	12,500	5	AT
*TOTAL PRIORITY 5						.75	37,500		
*TOTAL DEPARTMENT 01						2.90	140,000		
6	92	34	202-1	MAINTAIN BTAM	AT	.50	22,500	6	AT
		35	201-1	MAINTAIN SCP	AT	2.00	100,000	6	AT
*TOTAL PRIORITY 6						2.50	122,500		
3	92	35	201-2	INSTALL VM	ABOVE	2.00	100,000	3	ABOVE
			202-2	LOCAL VTAM	ABOVE	.50	25,000	3	ABOVE
			202-3	REMOTE VTAM	AT	.38	18,750	3	AT
*TOTAL PRIORITY 3						2.88	143,750		
2	91	34	143-1	MAINTAIN DYL250	BELOW	.20	9,000	2	BELOW
*TOTAL PRIORITY 2						.20	9,000		
*TOTAL DEPARTMENT 02						5.57	275,250		
TOTAL						8.47	415,250		

Figure 7.7.

5. Activities over $100,000

Content: Key information about all activities with a total cost of over $100,000 or other such amount.

Sequence: Priority, Cost, Activity Number (all grade levels are combined).

Totals: Priority.

Purpose: To segregate those very large projects that may need higher management approval.

6. New Activities

Content: Key information about all activities that are above current levels of involvement.

Sequence: Priority, Activity Number (all grade levels combined).

Totals: Priority.

Purpose: To identify those activities to be added to the current workload and that may require scrutiny by the user steering committee.

7. Activities to be Dropped

Content: Key information about all activities that are coded below current levels of involvement.

Sequence: Ascending Priority, Activity Number.

Totals: Priority.

Purpose: To identify those activities that will no longer be performed.

8. Deleted Activities by Sponsor

Content: Key information about all activities that are coded below current levels of involvement.

Sequence: Ascending Priority, Activity Number.

Totals: Priority.

Purpose: To make it perfectly clear to the sponsor which activities will not be supported next year.

9. Return on Investment (ROI)

Content: Important information about all activities. ROI is the quotient of the total amount saved per year times the expected life of the system divided by the cost to develop.

Sequence: ROI, Descending Priority.

Totals: Grand.

Purpose: To identify those activities with high ROIs that should be approved and those with low ROIs that perhaps should not be approved.

10. Man-loading Chart

Content: Activities with priorities 4, 5, and 6 for each grade level plotted against time. Separate graphs for each grade level and a combined graph for each department.

Sequence: Department, Grade Level.

Purpose: To identify peak periods of activities that may require rescheduling of some activities to a slower period or a higher staffing level with "fill in" activities from the priority 3 category.

11. Activity Package

Figure 7.8.

Purpose: This report is essentially a dump of the data base although selective decoding of symbols is advantageous. The example shown printed each activity on a separate page which allows selective updating of individual pages. This method does initially use up more paper, however. Although printing three or four activities on one page saves paper and makes updating easier, it requires a complete reprinting of all packages when any activities are added or deleted.

The FOCUS programs used to produce the reports above are included in Figure 7.9 through 7.13.

```
                                        ACTIVITY MASTER LIST
NUMBR
-----
105-1  ACTIV NAME  MAINTAIN P/R     PRIORITY  6  DEPARTMENT  01

       SAVINGS  100,000  START DATE  01/01/76  END DATE  12/31/78

       DEPENDENCIES  NONE          GRADE  34  MANDAYS    200

       CONTIN/PROJ  C  CURRDESC  AT     SPONNAME  ACCOUNTING

       ACTIV DESC  PROVIDE SYSTEMS AND PROGRAMMING SUPPORT FOR MAINTAING THE MSA PAYROLL SYSTEM

       OBJECTIVES  PROVIDE EFFIECIENT AND ACCURATE PAYROLL PROCESSING

       ACTIV SCOPE  MSA PAYROLL AND GENERAL LEDGER INTERFACE

       ADVANTAGES  MAINTAIN CONTROL OVER PROCESS AND KEEP IT IN HOUSE

       DISADVANTAGE  CONFIDENTIALITY

       ALTERNATIVES  HIRE SERVICE BUREAU

       CONSEQUENCES  NONE

134-5  ACTIV NAME  BILLING SYSTEM   PRIORITY  6  DEPARTMENT  01

       SAVINGS    5,000  START DATE  01/01/78  END DATE  12/31/78

       DEPENDENCIES  1344          GRADE  35  MANDAYS    230

       CONTIN/PROJ  P  CURRDESC  ABOVE  SPONNAME  ACCOUNTING

       ACTIV DESC  COMPUTER BILLING SYSTEMS DESIGN

       OBJECTIVES  IMPLEMENT SOFTWARE PHYSICS THEORY

       ACTIV SCOPE  ALL USERS OF THE DATA CENTER

       ADVANTAGES  MORE ACCURATE METHOD OF ALLOCATING EXPENDITURES

       DISADVANTAGE  DIFFICULT TO COMPREHEND SOFTWARE PHYSICS CONCEPTS

       ALTERNATIVES  DO NOTHING AND STAY WITH PACES

       CONSEQUENCES  NONE
```

Figure 7.8.

```
                                                  ACTIVITY MASTER LIST
NUMBR
-----
141-1  ACTIV NAME  MAINTAIN G/L     PRIORITY  5  DEPARTMENT  01

       SAVINGS   10,000  START DATE  01/01/78  END DATE  12/31/78

       DEPENDENCIES  0000          GRADE  35  MANDAYS    100

       CONTIN/PROJ  C  CURRDESC  AT     SPONNAME  ACCOUNTING

       ACTIV DESC  MAINTAIN VENDOR GENERAL LEDGER PACKAGE

       OBJECTIVES  KEEP PACKAGE CURRENT

       ACTIV SCOPE  PACKAGE USERS

       ADVANTAGES  MAINTAIN CURRENT VENDOR CODE

       DISADVANTAGE  NONE

       ALTERNATIVES  DO NOT MAINTAIN.  DO NOT UPDATE SOFTWARE WITH ENHANCEMENTS

       CONSEQUENCES  LIVE WITH EXISTING SYSTEM CAPABILITIES OR ELIMINATE SYSTEM

142-1  ACTIV NAME  MAINTAIN A/P     PRIORITY  5  DEPARTMENT  01

       SAVINGS    8,000  START DATE  10/10/78  END DATE  12/31/78

       DEPENDENCIES  0000          GRADE  35  MANDAYS     50

       CONTIN/PROJ  C  CURRDESC  AT     SPONNAME  ACCOUNTING

       ACTIV DESC  MAINTAIN ACCOUNTS PAYABLE PACKAGE

       OBJECTIVES  REMAIN CURRENT WITH VENDOR SUPPORT AND ENHANCEMENTS

       ACTIV SCOPE  A/P USERS

       ADVANTAGES  COST EFFICIENT

       DISADVANTAGE  NONE

       ALTERNATIVES  RETAIN CURRENT PACKAGE CAPABILITIES OR DO IT MANUALLY

       CONSEQUENCES  NONE
```

Figure 7.8 cont'd.

```
                                        ACTIVITY MASTER LIST
NUMBR
-----
143-1  ACTIV NAME  MAINTAIN DYL250  PRIORITY  2  DEPARTMENT  02

       SAVINGS         0  START DATE  01/01/78  END DATE  12/31/78

       DEPENDENCIES  NONE          GRADE  34  MANDAYS     40

       CONTIN/PROJ  C  CURRDESC  BELOW  SPONNAME  PROGRAMMING

       ACTIV DESC  MAINTAIN THE DYL250 SOFTWARE PACKAGE

       OBJECTIVES  KEEP PRODUCT CURRENT

       ACTIV SCOPE  DYL250

       ADVANTAGES  NONE

       DISADVANTAGE  OUT OF DATE PRODUCT

       ALTERNATIVES  USE DYL260

       CONSEQUENCES  NONE

201-1  ACTIV NAME  MAINTAIN SCP     PRIORITY  6  DEPARTMENT  02

       SAVINGS         0  START DATE  01/01/78  END DATE  12/31/78

       DEPENDENCIES  NONE          GRADE  35  MANDAYS    400

       CONTIN/PROJ  C  CURRDESC  AT     SPONNAME  TECH SERVICES

       ACTIV DESC  SUPPORT THE MVS OPERATING SYSTEM

       OBJECTIVES  MAINTAIN A FUNCTIONING SYSTEM

       ACTIV SCOPE  ALL IBM SUPPLIED SORTWARE NEEDED BY THE SYSTEM CONTROL PROGRAM

       ADVANTAGES  MAINTAIN OPERABILITY

       DISADVANTAGE  CONTINUED COST

       ALTERNATIVES  NONE

       CONSEQUENCES  SYSTEM WILL EVENTUALLY STOP OPERATING AND WILL NOT BE REPAIRED
```

Figure 7.8 cont'd.

```
                                        ACTIVITY MASTER LIST

NUMBR
-----
201-2  ACTIV NAME  INSTALL VM       PRIORITY  3  DEPARTMENT  02

       SAVINGS        0  START DATE  07/01/78  END DATE  12/31/78

       DEPENDENCIES  NONE          GRADE  35  MANDAYS    400

       CONTIN/PROJ  P  CURRDESC  ABOVE  SPONNAME  TECH SERVICES

       ACTIV DESC  INSTALL AND CONVERT OPERATING SYSTEM TO VM

       OBJECTIVES  UPGRADE OPERATING SYSTEM

       ACTIV SCOPE  ALL OPERATING AND APPLICATION SOFTWARE

       ADVANTAGES  REMAIN STATE OF THE ART

       DISADVANTAGE  NO INITIAL PAYBACK

       ALTERNATIVES  STAY WITH MVS

       CONSEQUENCES  POTENTIAL LOSS OF IBM SUPPORT IN THE FUTURE

201-1  ACTIV NAME  MAINTAIN BTAM    PRIORITY  6  DEPARTMENT  02

       SAVINGS  100,000  START DATE  01/01/78  END DATE  12/31/78

       DEPENDENCIES  NONE          GRADE  34  MANDAYS    100

       CONTIN/PROJ  C  CURRDESC  AT     SPONNAME  TECH SERVICES

       ACTIV DESC  MAINTAIN THE BTAM TELECOMMUNICATIONS PROTOCOL

       OBJECTIVES  MAINTAIN TELECOMMUNICATION OPERABILITY

       ACTIV SCOPE  ALL TP SOFTWARE

       ADVANTAGES  MAINTAIN OPERABILITY

       DISADVANTAGE  SOFTWARE OUT OF DATE

       ALTERNATIVES  CONVERT TO VTAM

       CONSEQUENCES  NO TELEPROCESSING
```

Figure 7.8 cont'd.

```
                                        ACTIVITY MASTER LIST
NUMBR
-----
202-2  ACTIV NAME  LOCAL VTAM       PRIORITY  3  DEPARTMENT  02

       SAVINGS  150,000  START DATE  10/01/78  END DATE  12/31/78

       DEPENDENCIES  NONE          GRADE  35  MANDAYS    100

       CONTIN/PROJ  P  CURRDESC  ABOVE  SPONNAME  TECH SERVICES

       ACTIV DESC  INSTALL LOCAL VTAM

       OBJECTIVES  UPGRADE SOFTWARE

       ACTIV SCOPE  ALL TELECOMMUNICATIONS SOFTWARE IN THE BUILDING

       ADVANTAGES  MAINTAIN STATE OF THE ART

       DISADVANTAGE  NONE

       ALTERNATIVES  STAY WITH BTAM

       CONSEQUENCES  NONE

202-3  ACTIV NAME  REMOTE VTAM      PRIORITY  3  DEPARTMENT  02

       SAVINGS    5,000  START DATE  06/01/78  END DATE  09/15/78

       DEPENDENCIES  NONE          GRADE  35  MANDAYS     75

       CONTIN/PROJ  P  CURRDESC  AT     SPONNAME  TECH SERVICES

       ACTIV DESC  INSTALL VTAM FOR REMOTE USERS

       OBJECTIVES  INSTALLATION OF REMORE VTAM

       ACTIV SCOPE  ONLY ONE DIVISION AFFECTED

       ADVANTAGES  IMPROVED FUNCTIONALITY AT THE REMOTE SITE

       DISADVANTAGE  NONE

       ALTERNATIVES  DO NOTHING

       CONSEQUENCES  NONE
DATE REVISED 07/01/78
```

Figure 7.8 cont'd.

```
DEFINE FILE ACTIVITY
CURRDESC/A5 = DECODE CURR(A 'ABOVE' T 'AT' B 'BELOW');
DEPTNAME/A13 = DECODE DEPT(01 'PROGRAMMING' 02 'TECH SERVICES'
           03 ' OPERATIONS' 04 'QUAL ASSUR');
SPONNAME/A13 = DECODE SPONSOR(01 'ACCOUNTING' 02 'MARKETING'
           91 'PROGRAMMING' 92 'TECH SERVICES');
NUMBR/A5 = EDIT(ACTNO,'999-9');
FTE/D6.2C = MANDAYS / 200;
COST/17C = IF GRADE='35' THEN MANDAYS*50000/200 ELSE
           IF GRADE='34' THEN MANDAYS*45000/200 ELSE 0;
END
SET WIDTH=132
TABLE FILE ACTIVITY
HEADING CENTER
"ACTIVITY CONTROL LIST"
" "
SUM ACTNA AS 'ACTIVITY NAME'
    CURRDESC AS 'AT ABOVE OR,BELOW CURRENT'
    FTE
    COST
    PRTY
    SPONNAME
    DEPEND
BY NUMBR
    BY DEPTNAME
    BY GRADE
END
```

Figure 7.9.

```
DEFINE FILE ACTIVITY
CURRDESC/A5 = DECODE CURR(A 'ABOVE' T 'AT' B 'BELOW');
DEPTNAME/A13 = DECODE DEPT(01 'PROGRAMMING' 02 'TECH SERVICES'
           03 ' OPERATIONS' 04 'QUAL ASSUR');
SPONNAME/A13 = DECODE SPONSOR(01 'ACCOUNTING' 02 'MARKETING'
           91 'PROGRAMMING' 92 'TECH SERVICES');
NUMBR/A5 = EDIT(ACTNO,'999-9');
FTE/D6.2C = MANDAYS / 200;
COST/17C = IF GRADE='35' THEN MANDAYS*50000/200 ELSE
           IF GRADE='34' THEN MANDAYS*45000/200 ELSE 0;
END
SET WIDTH=132
TABLE FILE ACTIVITY
HEADING CENTER
"HEADCOUNT RECONCILIATION - AT & BELOW CURRENT LEVELS"
" "
"DEPARTMENT: <DEPTNAME"
" "
SUM ACTNA AS 'ACTIVITY NAME'
    FTE AS 'FULLTIME,EQUIVALENT'
    COST
BY DEPT SUP-PRINT
    BY HIGHEST GRADE
    BY NUMBR
ON GRADE SUB-TOTAL
    ON DPET PAGE-BREAK
END
```

Figure 7.10.

```
DEFINE FILE ACTIVITY
CURRDESC/A5 = DECODE CURR(A 'ABOVE' T 'AT' B 'BELOW');
DEPTNAME/A4 = DECODE DEPT(01 'PGMG' 02 'TECH' 03 'OPER');
SPONNAME/A13 = DECODE SPONSOR(01 'ACCOUNTING' 02 'MARKETING'
           91 'PROGRAMMING' 92 'TECH SERVICES');
NUMBR/A5 = EDIT(ACTNO,'999-9');
FTE/D6.2C = MANDAYS / 200:
```

Figure 7.11.

```
COST/17C = IF GRADE='35' THEN MANDAYS*50000/200 ELSE
           IF GRADE='34' THEN MANDAYS*45000/200 ELSE 0;
END
SET WIDTH=132
TABLE FILE ACTIVITY
HEADING CENTER
"ACTIVITIES BY SPONSOR"
"DEPARTMENT - <SPONNAME"
" "
SUM NUMBR ACTNA AS 'ACTIVITY NAME'
    CURRDESC AS 'AT ABOVE OR,BELOW CURRENT'
    FTE AS 'FULL TIME,EQUIVALENT'
    COST DEPTNAME
BY SPONSOR SUP-PRINT
    BY HIGHEST PRTY
    BY NUMBR SUP-PRINT
ON PRTY SUB-TOTAL
    ON SPONSOR PAGE-BREAK
END
```

Figure 7.11. Continued.

```
DEFINE FILE ACTIVITY
CURRDESC/A5 = DECODE CURR(A 'ABOVE' T 'AT' B 'BELOW');
DEPTNAME/A13 = DECODE DEPT(01 'PGMG' 02 'TECH' 03 'OPER');
NUMBR/A5 = EDIT(ACTNO,'999-9');
FTE/D6.2C = MANDAYS / 200;
COST/17C = IF GRADE='35' THEN MANDAYS*50000/200 ELSE
           IF GRADE='34' THEN MANDAYS*45000/200 ELSE 0;
END
SET WIDTH=130
TABLE FILE ACTIVITY
HEADING CENTER
"ACTIVITIES BY DEPARTMENT"
"DEPARTMENT - <DEPTNAME"
" "
SUM NUMBR ACTNA AS 'ACTIVITY NAME'
    CURRDESC AS 'AT ABOVE OR,BELOW CURRENT'
    FTE
    COST
    PRTY
    CURRDESC
BY DEPT SUP-PRINT
    BY HIGHEST PRTY
    BY SPONSOR
    BY GRADE
    BY NUMBR SUP-PRINT
ON PRTY SUB-TOTAL
    ON DEPT PAGE-BREAK
END
```

Figure 7.12.

```
DEFINE FILE ACTIVITY
CURRDESC/A5 = DECODE CURR(A 'ABOVE' T 'AT' B 'BELOW');
SPONNAME/A13 = DECODE SPONSOR(01 'ACCOUNTING' 02 'MARKETING'
           91 'PROGRAMMING' 92 'TECH SERVICES');
NUMBR/A5 = EDIT(ACTNO,'999-9');
END
TABLE FILE ACTIVITY
HEADING CENTER
"ACTIVITY MASTER LIST"
" "
PRINT ACTNA AND PRTY AND DEPT OVER
```

Figure 7.13.

```
   SAVINGS AND START AND ENDDATE AND OVER
   DEPEND AND GRADE AND MANDAYS AND OVER
   CONT AND CURRDESC AND SPONNAME OVER
   DESC OVER
   SCOPE OVER
   ADVAN OVER
   DISADV OVER
   ALT OVER
   CONS
BY NUMBR UNDER-LINE
ON CONT SKIP-LINE
FOOTING
"DATE REVISED &DATE"
END
```

Figure 7.13. Continued.

8
Year-Long Uses for ZBB

By now, it should be obvious that using zero base budgeting techniques can be time consuming and labor intensive. This commitment can be quite costly if yours is a large MIS department with hundreds or even thousands of identifiable activities. On the positive side, from the use of ZBB in the planning process, you should be able to obtain a wealth of knowledge about your customers, a better understanding of the MIS department's activities, and other tangible benefits. This chapter identifies uses of the ZBB process throughout the rest of the year. Once the activity data base has been created and your staff is intimately familiar with the process, using it in other ways between annual budget cycles keeps the data base current and the staff organized. Think about it. If 90% of the ZBB process is spent creating the data base, the planning process during the second and subsequent years will be less labor intensive if that data base is kept up-to-date. The primary task will be limited to planning and decision making which are our main jobs anyway.

ZBB AND THE PROJECT CYCLE

It is short-sighted to assume that every single activity can be identified and fully documented over one year in advance. In a normal MIS environment, projects (activities) are requested every day, albeit most of them small, representing one or two days worth of effort. Some of these projects are even requested two days *after* they are needed by the end user and trying to operate in such dynamic environments can produce ulcers or at least a need for an occasional Tums. Avoiding this level of stress requires some forward planning and the continued use of the ZBB process.

Separating requests into logical groupings has worked at many surveyed companies:

- A trivial project is one that requires less than 5 man-days to complete. The specific number of days can vary between 3 and 10, depending on the workload, but should be formally stated and changed only infrequently. For example, setting a monetary cut-off of $1,000 can also be utilized as the equivalent of 5 man-days.
- Ongoing maintenance is covered in a blanket project for systems requiring regular and frequent maintenance such as a payroll system. A full-time equivalent, or a portion of one person's time, can be allocated to this task without having to constantly process trivial project requests. This blanket project should include such things as minor software updates and emergency production problems but not major system upgrades.
- Small projects are new systems or enhancements to old systems that are larger than trivial projects but less than six man-months long. They require a formal plan but, because their level of effort is in the $2,000 to $20,000 range, planning and control requirements placed upon the project should not be too burdensome.
- Large projects are new systems or enhancements that require more than six man-months and need extensive planning and control efforts.

During the annual planning process, a specific amount of staff time can be allocated for trivial projects because of their very nature. These projects are usually identified and executed on the spur of the moment and should not require upper management involvement. Specific zero base budgeting activities must be prepared for ongoing maintenance projects during the annual planning process. These projects require significant levels of effort and must be brought to the attention of management as a cost of doing business. The cost of operating the payroll system, for example, involves not just computer processing and data entry but also continual program maintenance. In organizations with a mature MIS function, system maintenance may entail from 50 to 70% of the total systems effort.

Small and large projects require special consideration, especially if they were not previously identified. New activities must be properly quantified and evaluated just like those identified in the annual planning process. An activity package must be prepared and a level of effort estimated with the same techniques used during the annual planning cycle.

Assuming that you have limited resources, there is no way that all new projects can be worked on in the current year. If they cannot wait until next year (and most of them cannot), the priority of each activity must be established and compared to the other approved activities. Perhaps the activity in question is more important and should replace one or more of the previously approved activities. Similarily, previously approved activities may need a higher priority because of changing business conditions.

In a normal project development environment, it is beneficial to place the burden of the decision making back onto the end user steering committee just as we did during the initial priority-setting process. Let the end users decide which projects will be accomplished and in what order. To this end, a User Advisory Committee should be formed. The members should be the same as those that participated in the ranking process described in Chapter 4. This committee has the charter to review projects and set their priorities throughout the year. Because the membership is the same as the original management committee, the advisory committee has the unique ability to view the big picture and provide a degree of continuity. The members of this committee are department/division managers and not senior-level managers. Senior-level managers should only be involved with the strategic plan approval process and the ranking and approval of very large projects over a stated amount, say, $100,000.

At a regular monthly meeting, the User Advisory Committee would be provided with decision packages prepared during the preceding month. These packages, along with an up-to-date set of staff utilization and availability reports, will enable the committee to set priorities for these activities properly thus providing guidance to the MIS manager.

The committee may elect to change the priority or sequence of any activities previously approved but not yet started. In this way, only the most important projects will be worked on.

The ranking process is exactly the same as described in Chapter 4 except that only proposed projects are acted upon by the committee. Projects in process and continuing activities are automatically accepted and cannot be discarded. The use of status reports and IBM cards or index cards, as described in Chapter 4, is very useful. Indicating staff schedules will help the committee understand priorities and the date a particular project can be completed.

It may be presumptuous to assume that all projects can wait until the next User Advisory Committee meeting. A procedure should be established for mid-month project approval in the case of emergencies. The User Advisory Committee chairman should be authorized to approve those really "hot" projects that cannot wait until the next formal meeting. The chairman should respond in a fair and equitable manner, treating each sponsoring department in a similar way, even his own. This procedure protects MIS management from organizational pressures and fills a loophole in the approval process.

THE INEVITABLE CHARGEBACK

An MIS department that does not allocate its expenditures back to the user departments/divisions may not find this section immediately useful, but when the time comes to establish greater control over the use of your data center, there are some valuable suggestions contained herein. Nolan's research indicates chargeback systems are usually introduced in stage III along with other management controls.

Theoretically, charging for services rendered is an excellent idea; practically speaking, it can be a nightmare. Although this section is not intended to be a treatise on computer billing systems, the adoption of some of the ideas presented here may help to alleviate your billing headaches. From a technical standpoint, any chargeback system can be implemented in a short period of time. The real failures are caused by political pressures and poor planning.

Why Chargebacks?

In order to effectively control data center operations, cost allocation is a necessity. If end users are not responsible for the cost of operating their systems, or are not even aware of the execution costs of their applications, there will be a significant waste of computer resources because of sloppy input, installation of marginally profitable systems, frivolous program changes, and arbitrary reruns. These users view the computer operation as a free service preferring to use the machine as an automated clerk that can spot errors and redo them. When machine cycles and labor are equated to billable dollars, the lost art of careful desk checking is quite often rediscovered. The chargeout/chargeback method makes the user community acutely aware of application operation costs. Not only are the costs demonstrated to them (chargeout) but payment is also required (chargeback), which forces them to budget funds. In very large companies with many legally separate divisions, the MIS invoice must be paid by check, which eliminates bookeeping headaches and also reinforces the chargeback philosophy. Computer operation costs are no longer regarded as an overhead expense when they become an item in the division's income statement rather than in the parent corporation's books.

Benefits Versus Drawbacks

When specifically addressing the benefits of chargeout and chargeback systems, a corresponding set of disadvantages can also be identified. What are some of the pros and cons relating to the allocations of MIS costs?

1. *Pro – User awareness and cooperation:* In the long run, user cooperation is enhanced by informing users of what they are paying for, down to the smallest detail if necessary. There arises a sudden zealousness to avoid duplication of charges due to oversight. Jobs are submitted with greater care and operational documentation is more accurate and complete when delays and reruns incur added costs. Intermediate job runs are no longer requested for the sake of curiosity. Methods of processing are fully evaluated in order to possibly alter the cost-effectiveness curve by taking advantage of economies of scale to give increased capability and decreased cost. With adequate education, the user thoroughly understands the measurement of use, unit rates, and resource charges. Data center and user personnel develop a rapport as cost reduction alternatives are discussed. Inefficient programs and clumsy job streams are scrutinized and modified in the interest of increasing benefits to the user.

   Con – User hostility and alienation. At best, it is difficult for the user to fully understand the nuances of a chargeout system. Oftentimes it seems as if the data center is attempting to cloak the computer in a shroud of mysticism. Chargeout documentation, which supposedly explains the methodology in plain language, is composed of esoteric algorithms referring to core resident hours or even units shipped. Terms are insufficiently defined and too technical. The user is forced to spend hours deciphering formulas only to arrive at a different cost for the job. It becomes nearly impossible for anyone without an advanced engineering degree to make a reasonably accurate estimate of the job's cost, especially when the actual charges vary from day to day. Additionally, rate and formula changes do not inspire confidence as the user begins to doubt the system's integrity. Of course, not all chargeback narrative is user-hostile. When the user frequently feels inadequate in attempting to intelligently calculate system costs, how can he be expected to estimate future run costs for budgeting current and new systems?

The opposite side of the issue is equally frustrating. A user may become disillusioned with data center operations when they are able to determine job costs coupled with bad service. Frequent down-time, inability to guarantee service levels and schedules, improperly prepared or lost reports, and rerun charges for errors beyond the control of the user, all contribute to the user's hostility toward the data center staff.

2. *Pro – Efficient use of MIS resources.* When user management is required to cost justify application expenses, they must also be able to quantify the benefits associated with the system. This leads to the elimination of marginally profitable applications or applications past their prime which makes available additional resource capacity. This also gives the user extra hardware capacity to support new systems and enhancements to existing systems. The data center is able to defer equipment orders without jeopardizing service levels simply because nonessential jobs have been dropped. By reducing operating costs and the frequency of hardware upgrades, the users will realize a benefit in the form of lower billing rates and less disruption of service usually associated with equipment installation.

   Con – Data center waste. Looking at computer use from a psychological standpoint, some people equate computing power and use with their personal egos. The more of it they use and the more it costs, the greater their sense of importance. Increased utilization of data center resources means increased organizational prominence. In this case, growing expenditures are not negatively perceived but, of course, promote wastefulness.

The perception that data centers are wasteful also stems from the excessive personnel time that chargeback systems are thought to require to update data bases with new software systems, additional hardware, and fluctuating rates. Overhead costs are also thought to be prohibitive because of the added administrative and operating expenses involved in running the system.

Quite naturally, when the user is responsible for costs, data center personnel may also become careless. Unless performance is closely monitored, sloppiness and indifference lead to unnecessary reruns, lack of coordination with users to ensure successful runs the first time, and less-than-optimal job scheduling and job mix.

3. *Pro – User criticism of data center expense.* A management information services department is traditionally viewed as a high overhead expense by users and chargeback systems make them more aware that processing costs are their responsibility and relate directly to their decisions. If users have a less expensive method of processing, they are welcome to use it. If not, criticism of expensive overhead is really criticism of their own inefficient decisions.

   Awareness of processing costs leads users to seek out alternative methods to obtain the same or increased benefits. By evaluating and improving computer performance, improving program code, and reconfiguring hardware, system costs can be minimized as processing is optimized.

   Con – Lower-priced services. Once users become aware of application costs, they are able to compare them against outside service prices. Sometimes they discover that outside processing can actually be cheaper. The difference may be small or large; however, a disgruntled user may be encouraged to utilize an outside service bureau if his frustration level is high enough. Usually the in-house facility can provide extra services such as quicker turnaround, rejected transaction correction, and faster reruns simply by virtue of its physical proximity. However, the possibility does exist that the data center could lose business once the user is fully apprised of costs.

Chargeback Methodologies

There are three methods of chargeback. The simplest method is to establish user fees by dividing your monthly budget by the number of users. This never works merely because some users will use your services more than others and the resulting charge is not equitable. Taking forecasted service levels for each user into account will provide a much more equitable allocation. However, this procedure still leaves a lot to be desired. Even if the predicted levels are based on last year's actual use and this year's planned MIS expenditures, the system lacks the ability to control reruns and provide timely accountability for use. The third method of chargeback, based on actual use, is by far the most equitable but also the most difficult to measure, understand, and operate. Perhaps a few examples might better explain the concept. All of these examples are based on true occurrences at companies in the greater Los Angeles area.

1. A $300 million, multidivisional company is comprised of 2 large divisions and 10 smaller ones. The annual budget is divided into two broad categories: operations and development. The development category consists of the salaries for all programmers, systems analysts, and their management plus expenses directly attributable to the group. All other expenses are included in the operations budget including software support, quality assurance, and MIS management.

   Development expenses are allocated based on actual hours expended on each project at a preset hourly rate. A list of major projects and their associated budgets are included in each division's annual plan except those divisions whose profit margin is too small to justify the expense. Operations expenses are budgeted based upon the division's prior year's use plus a "fudge" factor that compensates for the operation of new systems and expected increases/decreases in the actual use of existing systems.

The actual monthly charge for operations is the budgeted amount plus any variances (usually positive). The divisions prefer this method of chargeback because they can usually forecast the size of the charge. The charge for development varies from month to month based on actual hours. The divisions have greater control over the charge by choosing to accelerate or defer selected projects. Occasionally, the size of the charge comes as a surprise to the division but is not ordinarily a concern until the end of the year when their budgets run out. Further complicating the process are special "deals" worked out with the smaller divisions which result in fixed charges for selected projects or no charge at all for development and technical consulting.

Generally, this method works well for the company because it is suited to the informal nature of its environment. Occasionally, however, an allocation of computer resources is rejected by a division as having no basis in fact or because it cannot afford it.

2. A computer service bureau, which is a wholly owned subsidiary of a $4 billion conglomerate, provides a central computer resource for the other divisions. Services provided include computer processing, telecommunications, a private telephone network, and technical consulting. Systems development is decentralized in each division, although the computer division has a small systems staff to maintain a few common financial systems and to provide internal development needs.

   The costs incurred by this division are allocated entirely by computer use. Until 1981, these charges were based on *occupancy hours* which is a method whereby the total job processing time for each device is computed and then multiplied by a predetermined device rate. For example, a report that took 1 hour to run may have been "active" for only 6 minutes and swapped out for the other 54 minutes. The charge consists of the following factors:

Job-charge = Tape rate × .10 hours +
Tape-mount rate × 1 mount +
CPU rate × .005 CPU hours +
Line rate × 2,000 printed lines +
Core use rate × .10 hours

In 1981, the allocation system was completely changed from an actual-costs-incurred basis to independent revenue-producing formulas that support general corporate objectives. In order to meet a specific objective to lower personnel costs, jobs that operate without intervention carry a lower charge. For example, a job running as batch with no tapes and no printed output carries a cheaper rate than a job that requires an operator to mount tapes and burst the output. The charge for printed output was raised drastically to eight cents per page in order to encourage each division to obtain its own remote printers and reduce the computer center's labor-intensive processes and report delivery delays. Computer use is measured in terms of the number of bytes transferred (read or written) to each device plus CPU utilization adjusted by the individual machine's relative power. Further, an allowance for job abends is taken into account. Abends attributable to the computer center, such as I/O errors and the like, are not billed to the division. Division errors, such as data exceptions, are billed normally.

Complicating this process is an additional billing methodology, for selected applications that is based on the idea of a *natural business unit* (NBU). The theory is that end users do not comprehend "bytes transferred" or "occupancy hours" but do understand their own business. Therefore, why not charge for the operation of a payroll system based on the number of employees paid? Why not charge for the processing of invoices based on the number of invoices? Theoretically, this is an excellent method of computer chargeback because everyone can understand it. However, the development of the NBU rates is very complicated and can be risky because actual use may fall short of budgeted revenues. The MIS department must act just as if they are in business for themselves and selling a product rather than being a mere cost center.

Needless to say, the new system took over two years to implement because of its complexity and the amount of education required by the end user community. Even the technical staff in the other divisions had difficulty comprehending these new concepts.

3. A second computer service bureau, organized very similarly to the one above, allocates its computer operations expenses by occupancy hours with additional charges for dedicated hardware. Each division possesses *remote job entry* equipment for job submission and report printing. Data entry and data control are the responsibility of every division. Systems development, which is centralized, is absorbed by the parent corporation and not directly allocated to the operating divisions in order to encourage the development of common systems that are cheaper in the long run. Special requests for programming maintenance and other systems support is billed directly to the requesting division.

Each of these cases describes a particular method of allocating MIS costs. Popular job-accounting systems are available from many sources including the following:

- Compute-A-Charge – Value Computing
- Kommand – PACE Applied Technology
- Systems Management Facility – IBM Corporation
- CA-Jasper/JA – Computer Associates
- Control/IMS/CICS/SNF – Boole and Babbage, Inc.

Undoubtedly there are many more ways of allocating expenses and most of these packages can be tailored to the specific needs and policies of the company. A chargeout methodology always works in theory. Whether or not it is practical is another issue. Most allocation methodologies are politically motivated, and careers have been damaged in the process.

All of the allocation methods outlined above lack adequate accountability to a predetermined plan. In most cases, the accountability is limited to one or two budget line items for each division or user department and possibly supported by job run cost data.

Full accountability requires detailed information by each major category showing original plan, actual charges, and a forecast of future charges. Publishing these statistics requires a certain level of maturity as it may prove to be initially embarrassing to admit to a cost overrun or a bad estimate. The alternatives are worse, however. By not admitting a problem early on or by covering up inefficiencies, the problem only worsens and magnifies with the passage of time. Being secretive also adds to the DP mystique which does no one any good.

The zero base budgeting data base can provide the basis for a fully accountable allocation system. If the ZBB process is conducted properly initially, the data base will contain information about every activity that MIS is engaged in. If the ZBB process is utilized for project requests, as described above, or is at least updated with information about new projects, it can become the foundation for the chargeout system by providing the following useful information:

- A comprehensive activity list
- Budgeted manpower and dollars
- Start and end dates
- Sponsoring departments

By merging machine use charges and staff hours, a complete picture can be presented to the end user together with his invoice. Figures 8.1 and 8.2 are examples of such a reporting scheme. Figure 8.1 is a detailed invoice that includes forecasts of remaining charges based on estimates by your staff that prepare the user for potential budget overruns. Figure 8.2 details actual computer runs that support the invoice line items. The user now has enough information to make accurate decisions regarding his use of the MIS facility.

Full dependence on zero base budgeting requires the on-going maintenance of each user's activity catalog (see Chapter 4). The book must be kept up-to-date throughout the year as new activities for the department are identified. (In the long run, an up-to-date activity catalog eliminates substantial effort during the planning cycle.) The user has available a reference book that explains what the activity includes and whether or not it is worthwhile. If existing

MIS CHARGEOUT REPORT FOR JULY

Payroll Department

Activity No.	Activity Name	Actual Charges Current	Actual Charges YTD	Projected Charges Forcast	Projected Charges Total	Projected Charges Plan	Var	%
342-1	Weekly Payroll	1,700	12,000	12,000	24,000	20,000	4,000-	20-
343-1	941A Reports	536	1,000	1,000	2,000	2,400	400	18
384-1	W-2 Forms	0	0	1,500	1,500	1,500	0	0
	. . .							
Total operations		85,000	501,000	495,000	996,000	990,000	6,000	1
105-1	Maintain P/R	3,400	24,400	20,000	44,400	45,000	600	13
126-2	Rewrite Time Cd	2,000	2,000	9,000	11,000	10,000	1,000-	10-
130-2	Enhance Comm.	0	5,000	0	5,000	5,000	0	0
	. . .							
Total Development		12,000	75,500	70,500	146,000	140,000	6,000-	4-

Figure 8.1.

DAILY JOB ACCOUNTING LOG

DEPT: Payroll

Date: 07/12/82

Activ	Job	Start	Elapsed	CPU Cost	Tape	Disk	Print	Total
342-1	PR201	15.00.00	00.45.30	22.17	6.60	45.65	21.88	96.30
	PR205	15.45.35	01.31.09	177.33	56.79	134.50	.90	369.52
	PR210	18.05.05	00.20.15	14.31	3.30	20.03	193.45	231.09
Total Activity 342-1								$ 696.91
343-1	PR301	04.00.15	00.25.14	43.89	3.30	30.06	2.50	79.75
	PR302	04.26.49	01.55.38	266.50	6.60	127.99	55.00	456.09
Total Activity 343-1								$ 535.84

Figure 8.2.

activities are to be replaced with those of a similar nature, the user has a head start in the decision-making process. However, the elimination of an approved activity, without replacement, should be agreed to with caution. Unless a suitable substitute activity can be identified, the elimination could result in unallocated MIS expenses which might require a modification of your rates or a reduction in expenditures. Both of these are crises if they occur in the middle of the year.

MANAGEMENT BY OBJECTIVES

A great many companies utilize *management by objectives* (MBO) techniques in one form or another. MBO emphasizes the setting of objectives according to generalized corporate goals and is used as the basis for performance appraisals, salary increases, and bonuses. Although MBO may specify the resources required to accomplish any given result, it does not specify how the objectives will be attained. The individual's driving force is to satisfy the objective, sometimes at almost any cost. But the ends do not necessarily justify the means. In the final analysis, what has been gained?

An additional problem with MBO is that overall corporate objectives are not always communicated downward and managers may not publish their own MBOs for their staff on a timely basis, if at all. This lack of communication defeats the whole purpose. How can we even conceptualize management objectives unless we understand what the big picture is? How can I make my manager look good if I don't know how he is measured and rewarded?

Utilizing the concepts contained in this book can help solve these deficiencies. Chapter 1 described how to prepare a strategic plan. If your plan follows the outline presented, it will contain not only the overall company objectives but the primary objectives of every department and/or division, including your own. A complete analysis of the problems and proposed solutions should be included in each department's strategic and operational plan.

Zero base budgeting is an obvious complement to MBO and will go a long way toward solving the first deficiency earlier identified. ZBB activities must be defined to meet some overall company objective. They not only describe what objectives are to be met but also how they will be met. There are many ways to accomplish every goal, but each one requires different resources and levels of effort. The ZBB structure lends itself very nicely to the process of choosing alternative ways of satisfying an objective.

For example, if we operate as a data processing service bureau serving the needs of the other divisions, one of the company's objectives is to charge back the expenses to those divisions on an equitable basis. In the examples shown in earlier chapter, three alternatives for accomplishing the chargeout of MIS costs were presented. Activity 134-1 called for continued maintenance of the existing computer billing system. Based on occupancy time, the system has a certain amount of inflexibility that is not totally accurate and fair without a great many manual adjustments. Activity 134-2 described what was necessary to upgrade the existing software to provide additional features and become more flexible. Activity 134-3 specified a new computer billing system based on software physics technology and additionally removed the link between actual expenses incurred and the charges assessed for a given type of job.

The overall objective of a chargeback system can be met with any of the three proposed activities but each one has a different price tag and degree of flexibility and fairness. Choosing one of these three activities specifies how the objective will be accomplished and what are the resources required. Utilizing ZBB techniques also tends to minimize the communication problems of the MBO process. If the two are joined, the mere publication of the activity catalog tells everyone precisely how you will accomplish your objectives.

RESOURCE CONTROL

The two largest resources in a MIS department are the hardware and the staff. Access to the computer can be restricted with physical locks and data security packages but control also implies accountability. How are the resources really being used? Coding the ZBB activity number on the job card can be used to summarize processing charges which can then subsequently be compared to budgeted amounts (see Figure 8.2).

The control over staff activities is much more difficult. Recording their hours is just the beginning. The more hours recorded in a chargeback system, the greater your revenues. However, if the hours are not accurately obtained, the total project effort will be overstated and potentially embarrassing. There is no substitute for detailed project planning and reporting, short of time clocks. Zero base budgeting is not a cure all but by using the ZBB activity number as your project code to restrict all unapproved projects, a much greater degree of control is possible. The numbering scheme adds a certain amount of continuity within your own department and will aid in communicating with your user departments. A single four digit number can be used to identify an activity from proposal stage through approval, design, coding, testing, and, finally, full operation.

References

1. Austin, L. Allan, *Zero-Base Budgeting: Organizational Impact and Effects,* American Management Association, New York, 1977.
2. Austin, L. Allan and Logan M. Cheek, *Zero-Base Budgeting: A Decision Package Manual,* AMACOM, New York, 1979.
3. Bernard, D., J. C. Emery, R. L. Nolan, and R. H. Scott, *Charging for Computer Costs,* Petrocelli, New York, 1977.
4. Bigelow, R. P. and S. H. Nycum, *Your Computer and the Law,* Prentice-Hall, Englewood Cliff, N.J., 1976.
5. Buss, M. D., "Penny-wise Approach to Data Processing," *Harvard Business Review,* July–August, 1981.
6. Carter, Jimmy, *Budget Address to the Joint Session of the General Assembly of Georgia,* Atlanta, Georgia, January 13, 1972.
7. Carter, Jimmy, "On Zero-Base Budgeting," Interview held in the Governor's Office, Atlanta, Georgia, January 7, 1974.
8. Chambers, J. C., S. K. Mullick and D. D. Smith, "How to Choose the Right Forecasting Technique," *Harvard Business Review,* July–August 1971.
9. Cheek, Logan M., *Zero-Base Budgeting Comes of Age,* AMACOM, New York, 1977.
10. Cortada, James W., *EDP Costs and Charges,* Prentice-Hall, Inc., Englewood Cliffs, N.J., 1980.
11. Cushing, B., *Accounting Information Systems and Business Organizations,* Addison Wesley, Reading, Mass., 1982.
12. Davis, G. B., *Management Information Systems,* McGraw-Hill, Inc., New York, 1974.
13. Dean, Burton V., "Zero-Base Budgeting in Industry," Paper presented at the ORSA/TIMS Joint National Meeting, Atlanta, Georgia, November 1977.
14. Dillon, Ray D., *Zero-Base Budgeting for Health Care Institutions,* Aspen Systems Corporation, New York, 1979.
15. Ditri, A. E., J. C. Shaw, and W. Atkins, *Managing the EDP Function,* McGraw Hill, New York, 1971.
16. EDP Auditors Association, *Control Objectives,* (forthcoming) 1983.
17. Foy, N. S., *Computer Management: A Common Sense Approach,* Auerback Publishers, Phildelphia, 1972.
18. Francl, Thomas J., W. Thomas Lin, and Miklos A. Vasarhelyi, "ZBB Fits DP To a Tee," *Datamation,* September 1980.
19. Frank, Michael R., *The Effective EDP Manager,* AMACOM, New York, 1980.

20. Froehlich, A. F., *Managing the Data Center,* Wadsworth, Inc., 1982.
21. Hermanson, Roger H. and George S. Minmier, "A Look at Zero-Base Budgeting – The Georgia Experience," *Government Accountant's Journal,* Winter 1976.
22. Hill, W. D., *Implementing Zero-Base Budgeting,* The Planning Executives Institute, Oxford, Ohio, 1977.
23. Joslin, E. O., *Computer Selection,* Addison-Wesley, Reading, Mass., 1968.
24. Kanter, Jerry, "MIS Long Range Planning," *Infosystems,* June 1982.
25. Lin, W. Thomas, "Corporate Planning and Budgeting: An Integrated Approach," *Managerial Planning,* May/June 1979.
26. Long, Larry, *Design and Strategy for Corporate Information Services, MIS Long-Range Planning,* Prentice-Hall, Inc., Englewood Cliffs, N.J., 1982.
27. "Long Range and Strategic Planning For EDP," *The Institute for Management Automation,* January 1978.
28. Makridakis, S., and S. C. Wheelwright, *Forecasting: Methods and Applications,* John Wiley and Sons, New York, 1978.
29. McKell, L. J., J. V. Hansen, and L. E. Heitger, "Charging for Computer Resources," *Computing Surveys,* June 1979.
30. Nolan, Richard L., "Effects of Chargeout on User/Manager Attitudes," *Communications of the ACM,* March 1977.
31. Nolan, Richard L., "Computer Data Bases: The Future Is Now," *Harvard Business Review,* September–October 1973a.
32. Nolan, Richard L., "Managing the Computer Resource: A Stage Hypothesis," *Communications of the ACM,* vol. 16, no. 7, July 1973b.
33. Nolan, Richard L., "Managing the Crises in Data Processing," *Harvard Business Review,* March–April 1979.
34. Olson, M. H. and B. Ives, "Chargeback Systems and User Involvement in Information Systems – An Empirical Investigation," *MIS Quarterly,* June 1982.
35. Patillo, James W., *Zero-Base Budgeting: A Planning, Resource Allocation and Control Tool,* National Association of Accountants, New York, 1977.
36. Peat, Marwick, Mitchell and Co., "Zero-Base Budgeting Believed to Improve Current Budgeting Practices," *Managerial Planning,* July/August 1977a.
37. Peat, Marwick, Mitchell and Co., *ZBB in the Federal Government – Prospects for Success,* PMM and Co., New York, 1977b.
38. Phyrr, Peter A., "Zero-Base Budgeting," Speech delivered at the International Conference of the Planning Executive Institute, New York, May 1972.
39. Phyrr, Peter A., "Zero-Base Budgeting," John Wiley and Sons, Inc., New York, 1973.
40. Phyrr, Peter A., "Zero-Base Budgeting: Where to Use It and How to Begin," *SAM Advanced Management Journal,* summer 1976.
41. Ronen, J., and J. L. Livingstone, "An Expectancy Theory Approach to the Motivational Impacts of Budgets," *The Accounting Review,* October 1975.
42. Schaeffer, Howard, *Data Center Operations,* Prentice-Hall, Inc., Englewood Cliffs, N.J., 1981.

43. Shaw, J. C. and W. Atkins, *Managing Computer Systems Projects,* McGraw Hill, New York, 1970.
44. Schick, Allan and Robert Keith, "Zero-Base Budgeting," in U.S., Congress, Senate Committee on Government Relations, *Compendium of Materials on Zero-Base Budgeting in the States,* GPO, Washington, D.C., 1977.
45. Scott, Cowen, "The Use of Zero-Base Budgeting in States and Municipalities," Paper presented at the ORSA/TIMS Joint National Meeting, Atlanta, Georgia, November 1977.
46. Steiner, G. A., *Top Management Planning,* The MacMillan Co., New York, 1969.
47. Stibbens, S., "MIS Budgets are Dreams Until They are Funded," *InfoSystems,* June 1982.
48. Stonich, Paul J., *Zero-Base Planning and Budgeting,* Dow Jones-Irwin, Homewood, Ill., 1977.
49. Tourangeau, Kevin W., *The Canadian Zero-Base Budgeting Survey Report,* Touraine Publishing Corp., Toronto, 1979.
50. Vasarhelyi, M. A., "Man-Machine Planning Systems: A Cognitive Style Examination of Interactive Decision Making," Ph.D. dissertation, University of California, Los Angeles, 1973.
51. Welsch, G. A., *Budgeting: Profit Planning and Control,* Prentice-Hall, Inc., Englewood Cliffs, N.J., 1976.

Index